D0040823

DAMAGE NOTED

The Heartbeat at Your Feet

The Heartbeat at Your Feet

A Practical, Compassionate New Way to Train Your Dog

Lisa Tenzin-Dolma

ROWMAN & LITTLEFIELD PUBLISHERS, INC.
Lanham • Boulder • New York • Toronto • Plymouth, UK

Published by Rowman & Littlefield Publishers, Inc.
A wholly owned subsidiary of The Rowman & Littlefield Publishing Group, Inc.
4501 Forbes Boulevard, Suite 200, Lanham, Maryland 20706
www.rowman.com

10 Thornbury Road, Plymouth PL6 7PP, United Kingdom

British Library Cataloguing in Publication Information Available

Library of Congress Cataloging-in-Publication Data

Tenzin-Dolma, Lisa.
The heartbeat at your feet : a practical, compassionate new way to train your dog / Lisa Tenzin-
Dolma.
p. cm.
Includes bibliographical references and index.
ISBN 978-1-4422-1817-8 (cloth : alk. paper) — ISBN 978-1-4422-1819-2 (electronic)
1. Dogs—Training. 2. Dogs—Behavior. I. Title.
SF433.T467 2012
636.7'0887—dc23
2012022929

♾™ The paper used in this publication meets the minimum requirements of American
National Standard for Information Sciences Permanence of Paper for Printed Library
Materials, ANSI/NISO Z39.48-1992.

Printed in the United States of America

For my daughter, Amber Tenzin-Dolma

Contents

Acknowledgments

A great many people contributed to this book in some way—through asking for my help with their dogs, entering into discussions on the canine mind, test-reading, or reminding me that a mealtime had passed by some hours ago and I was still sitting at the computer. These are just a few of those to whom I owe heartfelt thanks.

Claire Gerus, my literary agent and an all-round wonder woman. My editor at Rowman & Littlefield , Suzanne Staszak-Silva, who commissioned this book and who patiently answered my technical questions about formatting. Kathryn M. F. Knigge, Suzanne's assistant editor. My students at the International School of Canine Psychology (ISCP), who are dedicated to putting the principles into daily practice and who are making such a difference to the public's perception of dogs.

My clients and their dogs, who provided me with many, many opportunities to see the beneficial results of the Sympatico method—and special thanks to those whose stories are shared in this book.

My expert test-readers and givers of valuable feedback—Theo Stewart, chair of the Association of INTO Dogs, provider of a daily fount of inspiration and humor, and an ISCP graduate; and Amelia Welham, my fabulous veterinary surgeon, who treats every animal with the utmost compassion and generously shares her extensive veterinary knowledge. Rachel Parnell, fosterer extraordinaire. Debby Lovell, who asked for (in her own words) the "oldest, ugliest dog" in rescue and adopted her. Jane Sigsworth, Sue Bosworth, and Pippa Woodward-Smith of the Association of INTO Dogs, who, with Theo and the other members, wholeheartedly promote positive methods. Beverley Cuddy, editor and publisher of *Dogs Today* magazine and champion of all dogs, especially the underdog.

My friends at the Oldies Club charity, especially Fiona Chalk, Sandra Simpson, Amy Jones, Elaine Wilkinson, Jeanne Stone, Victoria Clare, Angela Chapman, and Aura Beckhöfer Fialho, just some of the people who work tirelessly on behalf of senior dogs. And all the fosterers who take care of Oldies Club dogs, who share in celebrating each rehoming and support each other through the grief we all feel when a beloved dog passes away.

My dear friends Jen Govey, Carole Negre, Yolanda Cheung, Cheryl Stringall, and Tony Lowe, who have stuck around through numerous books and provided encouragement, delicious meals, uplifting music, and a great deal of laughter. Many thanks to Annie and Bryan Rawlings, who allowed me to write about their dogs in chapter 6: "Who's Training Whom?"

My family. My daughter, Amber, to whom this book is dedicated—she gives boundless unconditional love to every sad and sick dog who arrives at our home. My sister, Julie, who's always happy to spend hours talking about dogs. My sons—Ryan, Oliver, Daniel, and Liam—who never say, "What? Another dog?" My cousin and fellow dog enthusiast, Sue. My parents, who rehomed several unwanted dogs and instilled in me an enduring love for, and fascination with, our four-legged friends.

Every dog I have lived with and worked with has taught me a great deal—I'm grateful beyond words to all of them. Skye, my canine soul mate, helper, and mentor, welcomes each new dog with open paws and works his own brand of magic on them. Shep, "The Shepster," my elderly foster dog, is a supreme example of triumph over adversity and sheer dogged determination. And I treasure the memories of the dogs who brought so much joy during their too-short lives, and who will always hold a special place in my heart—Trixie, Zoe, Bobby, Kerry, Carnie, Orla, Lucy, and Tilly.

Foreword

At *Dogs Today* magazine we receive a copy of pretty much every book about dogs ever published. Many of them are obviously formulaic and lacking in knowledge, purpose, or passion. But every now and again a really great book comes along that delights and enlightens in equal measures. It is so obvious that Lisa has a great love and understanding of dogs, and through this book others too can better enjoy a more rewarding and positive relationship with their best friend.

I'd like everyone contemplating getting a dog to read this book.

When I asked Lisa about her motivation for writing this book, she said, "I love dogs and find them fascinating, and I feel strongly that the very special bond that exists between dogs and people should be honored and celebrated."

I am sometimes asked why my life has revolved around dogs, but it's usually someone who doesn't have a dog who asks me the question!

I've spent decades writing and campaigning to try to make things better for dogs for a very simple reason.

A dog named Sally let me into an amazing secret world. She showed me how completely amazing dogs can be. And when I saw that special something in Sally, I started seeing the potential in every dog's face. And it made me incredibly sad how many end up dead because people have messed them up and let them down.

Dogs can't talk; someone needs to speak up for them—to point out how incredibly special they are and how they deserve better.

We need books like these that tell us what dogs need to live alongside us harmoniously.

My dear friend and hero Dr. Ian Dunbar once said that there are only four things on the planet that instinctively love man no matter what he does: dogs, horses, dolphins, and women.

It's something we all probably take for granted—but shouldn't.

Unconditional love is so very rare, yet there are millions of dogs in Britain straining at the leash to deliver it.

If you have ever experienced the love of a good dog, you will know the power of it. It definitely changed me.

Almost twenty years ago my magazine, *Dogs Today*, had won its first award at the publishing equivalent of the Oscars, and one of the judges, the glamorous editor of a glossy women's magazine, asked me what my next career move would be. When would I be making the progression into "real" magazines?

She wasn't being intentionally rude. She didn't understand that I already had the very best job in the world. She'd obviously never loved and been loved by a dog. It's true my editor's freebies weren't Prada handbags and Jimmy Choos, but I had a connection with my readers that she'd probably kill for.

Dog lovers talk to each other in parks like old friends. They help each other without a second thought. They know what's important and it's certainly not designer labels.

My dog Sally taught me to love dogs, but everyone has their own first love story and they are all epic.

My family had lots of dogs around when I was growing up, possibly too many. I thought I loved dogs back then, but I was just a keeper of dogs. Our dogs loved each other and we fed, groomed, and planned their next generations, but we didn't spend much quality time together—there were just too many dogs and too little time to get close.

Sally changed everything.

When she was born I thought she was the most technically perfect Bearded Collie I had ever seen. Others probably just saw cute, but her perfectly arranged angles and proportions somehow dazzled me.

Back then vaccines were still very basic and she fell terribly ill from a ferocious new illness called parvovirus.

We were lucky to have had a brilliant young vet who had already seen lots of other pups die from this new disease. They'd go on a drip, get really depressed, and just give up.

My mum and I asked her what the best treatment was. What would the vet do if Sally was her dog?

She sent Sally home with instructions for us to syringe an electrolyte solution by mouth every fifteen minutes and to bring Sal back once a day for a painful injection that would hopefully slow down her vomiting long enough to stop her dying from dehydration.

We just had to keep her alive long enough to fight through the virus and away from all other dogs.

Parvo is a ghastly illness. It makes pups so sick that they pass blood—they can't keep anything down.

We already had a special room at home we used for rearing puppies and that became Sally's sick room.

She seemed happiest sitting on my lap and that close contact meant I could feel the very first spasm that signaled she was going to be violently sick. Next to me was a table and a book in which I'd record the time intervals between the liquid being syringed into her mouth and the inevitable retching.

I'd just finished my degree; I was waiting to start my first proper job. I had time on my hands so I could take this challenge on. My mum and dad said they would take over while I had a few hours' sleep, but between us we could theoretically maintain the fifteen-minute syringing regime, twenty-four hours a day, without ever having to leave poor old Sally alone on a drip in a cage at the vets.

Despite her illness, Sal was very good company.

She'd look me in the eye with the beautiful brown eyes and wag her now bedraggled tail whenever I spoke to her. I did spend a lot of time telling her that she was a very good dog and telling her all the things we'd do together when she got well.

I guess I didn't notice that I was falling in love with her. That she had changed from a valuable show dog into a totally priceless friend.

It wasn't the way she looked that had touched my heart—it was her indomitable spirit.

Every day she'd greet the vet with a lick—even though Sal knew she would administer an injection into the muscle that would really sting. We'd measure how poorly Sal was by the intensity of that cry. A quiet whimper meant we were probably losing the battle. A waiting-room-emptying scream meant it was a good day.

Sally was visibly shrinking.

She was only a few weeks old; she should have been eating four or five nutritious meals a day at this stage. Instead she was struggling to keep basic liquids down for more than a few minutes.

Her once teddy-bear-colored thick fur coat looked really dull and flat, and it was now obviously a size or two too big for her. She was just sparse fluff, skin, and bone.

I found I was wishing for a miracle but at the same time fearing the very worst.

Sally was such a brave little dog. Her eyes told me she didn't want to die. Her tail told me she wasn't giving up either.

The days became a week. While Sally wasn't giving up, I was close to it. Were we being cruel? Were we torturing her? How was this going to end?

She would see the tears in my eyes and she would comfort me—her selflessness made me even sadder!

The notebook was filling up with time intervals. The further away from the daily jab, the shorter the time the liquids stayed down.

Days and nights blurred and Sally and I got ever closer and closer and I was more and more terrified of losing her. Nothing outside of that room seemed to matter.

One day I assumed I'd just gotten overtired and confused and had not properly recorded the time she'd last been sick, but then she kept the next syringe full down, too.

I can't begin to explain the euphoria I felt at realizing we'd gotten our miracle.

She wasn't going to die.

I came out of that room changed forever.

I would do anything for Sally and she would do anything for me. We had a bond that would never break. When I looked into the dog's eyes, I saw so much more than I ever did before.

I had found my passion in life.

For the next sixteen years Sally filled my life with so much love.

It wasn't ever easy, though. This wasn't a soppy movie.

Her illness had meant she had missed out on all the necessary socialization that a dog needs. I was to discover that she was now afraid of everything and everyone apart from me. She suffered terrible separation anxiety, too.

If I left her side she would start passing blood again. If she was even slightly stressed she would poo.

She thought other dogs were an alien species and would bite them.

We had so many more battles ahead, but we fought on together using the gentlest possible methods.

By the time she was an old dog she was afraid of nothing, but still wanted to be by my side even if it meant carrying her up the stairs to bed each night.

The magazine was peppered with the stories of our struggles to achieve normality, of embarrassing slipups that still make me blush and terrible failures that would horrify a succession of boyfriends and their parents, and even meant I missed a vital meeting with the prime minister at 10 Downing Street!

But I wouldn't have missed a day or changed a thing.

Sally was also to battle and conquer numerous terrible health problems, but again she'd just look me firmly in the eye and we'd somehow get through it together.

It wasn't ever easy sharing my life with Sally—she was a very high maintenance dog—but they were the very best of times.

Sally made me aspire to be as brave as she was. With her at my side I felt I could do almost anything. And when I heard of a dog in trouble I felt I had to do something. Sally had opened a door that couldn't be closed.

Wherever Sal was, that was my home. She'd be asleep on my feet on long nights when I'd work late to get my dog magazine off the ground. I'd never have been brave enough to stay in that office late at night without her.

I can still see her lovely trusting face if I close my eyes. And remember the tears of the vet too when we said our good-byes for the final time.

I will never forget her or be able to thank her enough for introducing me to the secret world of dogs.

She taught me how to love, how to nurture, and that if you want something you have to fight for it and work at it.

Thankfully, not all dogs will have as many problems to overcome as Sally did, yet many thousands of owners will still give up at the first obstacle and never get to share the good times.

Young healthy dogs with so much love to give are put to sleep every day. People walk by and see the problems and not the potential.

I am hoping that this book will better prepare people for the journey ahead and help them avoid some of the bumps—and that fewer dogs will die still yearning to love someone.

Dogs are so patient and forgiving—they really do deserve so much better.

I am sure this book will help very many people better understand what that dog at their feet needs.

In the twenty-one years I have edited *Dogs Today*, I have met so many remarkable dogs. Dogs that have saved people's lives, saved their marriages, literally opened doors, and even operated cash machines.

I've also seen the numbers of healthy good dogs killed increase and seen society's tolerance of all dogs become tested as passive owners increasingly give dogs a bad name.

Dogs deserve so much more than this.

We need more people to see the world through dogs' eyes and try to change things.

I hope when you've finished reading and rereading the wise words in this book, you'll join us as a reader at *Dogs Today* magazine and help us try to change things for other dogs, too.

Beverley Cuddy, editor and publisher of *Dogs Today* magazine

Introduction

A New Rhythm

It's a fact: our bond with dogs can sometimes actually be easier and less "conditional" than our relationships with other people. After all, dogs are fully present in the moment and freely offer their undying affection, companionship, and devotion. They're always delighted to see us, they ask very little of us beyond fulfilling their basic needs, and they are great playmates. They also work hard on our behalf, taking on roles which include herding, guarding, saving lives, search and rescue, and helping those with disabilities.

Yet dogs are complex creatures, capable of far more than we often realize, and they have sophisticated communication methods that most of us are completely unaware of. This book reveals how you can truly understand your dog and experience a real deepening of your bond with your devoted fur-friend. Dogs understand us better than we think, and they observe us closely. In fact, dogs are expert anthropologists. As you will discover in the following chapters, they can read our facial expressions and body language and can sense the subtle chemical changes that occur in our bodies when we are afraid or upset. These abilities have been honed through thousands of years of evolving alongside us. This began as a survival mechanism, because our ancestors trained their dogs to be dependent upon them for food and shelter, and it developed further through dogs' desire to be close to us, as members of their social groups and as part of our families.

Until recently it was assumed that dogs were domesticated wolves, that they viewed us as pack members, and that we must constantly prove to them that we are the "top dog" or "alpha" by dominating them and using harsh punishment to keep them in their place. This theory was based on studies of managed captive wolf packs, which actually display very different behaviors from wolves in the wild. Scientific research, especially over the past ten years, has shown that dogs think and behave very differently from both wild and captive wolves.

Dogs were, in fact, the first animals to become domesticated. Their brains have become hardwired to associate with us as members of their social group, and they keep a close eye on us in order to interact with us as harmoniously as possible.

THE BACKSTORY: A DOG IS NOT A WOLF

The wolves that roam free nowadays are very different creatures to the original wolves of past millennia. They have evolved since the early times, just as dogs have, adapting to changes in the environment in order to survive.

Until recently researchers thought that a dog was a wolf in a new fur coat and that the behavior of dogs was based on the same social relationships, instincts, and drives as these distant ancestors. Therefore, we could use what was called "the wolf model" in order to better understand our canine friends. Because until recently it wasn't easy to study wild wolves, as they tend to avoid humans, groups of captive wolves were used as the basis for figuring out why dogs do what they do.

In the wild, wolf packs are composed of family groups: the parents (alphas) and their offspring. Only the parents mate because otherwise the risk of genetic disorders would be high. The cubs grow up with their families and stay, helping with the hunt and assisting in rearing the next litter of cubs, until they are mature enough to leave home, find a mate, and start their own packs.

Cooperation between pack members is vital because any serious conflict between them could endanger the survival of the entire pack. Arguments that arise are usually dealt with through posturing—rather like a human teenager who shouts and swaggers to make a point but soon backs down. The wolves look out for each other and take care of each other. The bonds they form are close, as you would expect with families, and the death of a pack member is often marked by group howling, revealing a close similarity to human grief. Wolves mark out large areas of territory and tend to be careful to avoid other packs.

Captive wolf packs, which the old behavior studies were based on, are very different. Unrelated wolves, who would normally carefully steer clear of each other, are put together in an enclosure from which they cannot escape. Their natural instinct to roam widely is curtailed, and they are trapped in each other's company. This leads to competition for resources—territorial space, food, and mates—and conflict can become vicious, with the strongest wolves engaging in combat. The harmony of the natural family unit is put seriously at risk.

Observations of captive wolf packs gave rise to the theory that, like these wolves, dogs were aggressive, dominance-driven creatures who constantly strove to be the "alpha" over other dogs and humans in their group and would take any steps necessary to achieve this. Recent research has proven this theory to be wrong.

HOW DOGS REALLY VIEW US

Dogs see us as members of their social group. They don't consider us to be rather odd-looking dogs. In your dog's eyes, you provide the shelter, food, and affection. You decide when your dog has a meal or gets attention or goes for a walk. In a sense, our dogs are willing prisoners who are dependent on us for their survival, who choose to live with us because they have evolved to desire that bond.

In return for a home with us, they give unstinting loyalty and devotion. They are not looking out to "dominate" us or to put themselves forward as leaders of the group. However, the world of the domesticated dog is fraught with dangers that they would not be able to easily interpret or circumnavigate. Dogs need us to be their guides and to teach them appropriate behaviors that keep them safe and allow us to enjoy their company. We can do this compassionately, through using positive methods that foster trust and strengthen the human-canine bond.

FROM WOLF TO DOG

The "wolf theory," which has been the foundation for understanding dogs for many years, postulated that wild wolves learned to live alongside humans and earned their food and shelter by helping with the hunt, pulling heavy loads, protecting livestock, and serving as lookouts for intruders. In their book, *Dogs: A Startling New Understanding of Canine Origin, Behavior, and Evolution*, behavioral biologists Raymond and Lorna Coppinger explore in detail why it's extremely unlikely that wolves would have easily settled into these new roles.[1]

Wolves, by nature, avoid humans. Their predatory instincts are too powerful to allow them to guard flocks. Their need for personal space, and dislike of being trapped in close proximity to others, could make their ability to pull a sled while lashed to teammates either ineffectual or potentially disastrous.

Dogs are team players and have a strong drive for social interaction both with other dogs and with humans. They willingly carry out designated tasks and strive to please us. Yet their DNA is 99.96 percent wolf, so how did their domestication and their bond with people come about?

LEARNING TO LIVE TOGETHER

Some of the wolves who usually avoided humans learned to overcome their shyness when the first human settlements sprang up. Communities of people meant the appearance of dump areas for waste products. In times when food was scarce, the boldest of the hungry wolves came closer in order to scavenge on the leftovers. As time passed, the offspring of the "dump" wolves had better chances of survival because a "ready meal" was close by, though it's very unlikely that there would have been enough leftovers to fully support large numbers of wolves. These wolves learned to more easily tolerate the presence of humans. It's likely that humans encouraged some to stay, by feeding them instead of driving them away, and then adopted wolf cubs, choosing the ones who were the friendliest, to play with and to provide an early warning system if intruders were in the area.

Through multiple generations of breeding from the tamest wolves, the early dogs came into being. It's thought that this first occurred between 12,000 and 14,000 years ago because of carbon-dated remains of domesticated dogs from that period. However, our relationship with our canine friends could stem back as far as 135,000 years, according to evidence from mitochondrial DNA.

MATERNAL HERITAGE

Mitochondria are located in the fluid that surrounds the nucleus of cells and provide energy to cells. Mitochondrial DNA (known as mtDNA) is passed on through the female line, from mother to offspring, and can be examined through the hair. The research into this resulted in a paper by Leonard, Wayne, Wheeler, Valadez, Guillén, and Vilà in *Science* magazine in 2002, which shows evidence that the early ancestors of dogs were European, not American, wolves and that this ancestry goes back much further than had been previously thought.[2]

This research, however, although it shows the link between European wolves and dogs, looks into the female lineage. Mitochondrial DNA can't tell us about the male ancestors, so it's likely that male American timber wolves would have mated with domestic dogs many thousands of years ago. Certainly this does happen now and results in wolf hybrids.

EVOLUTION

Through closer proximity with humans, the fear that prevented wild wolves from approaching people lessened. This meant that levels of adrenaline, the chemical that stimulates the "freeze, flight, or fight" instinct, became lower. As an offshoot of this, eventually other changes took place. The skull and teeth became smaller. There were changes in coat colors and textures, and the early dogs learned that bonding with the humans who cared for them brought rewards in the form of food, shelter, and company.

Selective breeding, through choosing the animals who were amenable, willing to pay attention to their human companions, and able to follow through on specific tasks, set the scene for the multitude of dog breeds that we see today.

HOW DO WE KNOW THIS?

In the 1950s a series of experiments began that are still in operation today. They concern silver foxes, not dogs, but they have changed the way that scientists view dog evolution.[3]

Russian scientist Dmitry Konstaninovich Belyaev was called in to work on a Russian fur farm where the silver foxes, which were being bred for their fur, were too vicious toward humans to be easily handled. Belyaev chose the least fearful and aggressive of the silver foxes and bred them, going on to choose the tamest of their offspring for breeding, and so on through the generations. After thirty generations and forty years, the breeders noticed marked changes. Many of these new-breed silver foxes looked and behaved more like dogs. Their coats changed, their ears were floppier, they made barking sounds—and they were friendly and affectionate toward humans.

Tests showed that these tame foxes had lower levels of adrenaline in their systems. This lessening of the fear and aggression chemical brought about other chemical changes too, such as changes in melanin, which governs coat color (and skin color in humans).

Dogs are not silver foxes, but the Russian experiments give strong pointers to how dogs evolved from domesticated wolves many thousands of years ago. Our ancestors brought home wolf pups and selectively bred the pups that showed the most potential for tameness, willingness to interact, and ability to carry out tasks.

So dogs started off as domesticated wolves and evolved through long association with humans. Their DNA is still very close to that of wolves, but their behavior is very different. Recently, scientists such Dr. John Bradshaw have discovered through their research that DNA does not determine behavior.[4] We couldn't call a dog a type of wolf, any more than we could call a wolf a type of dog!

THE HEARTBEAT AT YOUR FEET

Dogs were the first animals to be domesticated, and they have lived with us, kept us company, and worked alongside us for many thousands of years. During this time they have learned even more about us than we have about them—though the recent research results into how dogs think, and into why they react and respond as they do, have now made it far easier for us to understand the dog mind and to develop relationships with them that have a stronger foundation. Dogs' brains have become hardwired to associate with us as members of their social group (their family). Their extraordinary senses have been tapped so that we can even employ them to sniff out cancer cells. Their acute observation of us has enabled us to train them for particular tasks—and to teach them tricks for our own entertainment. And their desire to live harmoniously with us has brought us the devotion and affection of constant, unconditional companionship and friendship.

The heartbeat of the dog drums a rhythm that is uniquely in harmony with our own.

The Heartbeat at Your Feet takes you on a journey through the mind of your dog and shows how this impacts on his relationship with you. Along the way you will discover how your dog experiences the world, and this may lead you to look at your dog from a new perspective. Descriptions of some common behavior issues, and ways in which you can remedy these, are included, along with lots of personal stories that illustrate the very special bonds we have with our furry friends. As a canine psychologist I use, and recommend, only positive, compassionate methods, because our relationships with our dogs should be based on trust, not fear. I call these methods "Sympatico," from the Italian "simpatico," which means "sympathy." In order to develop a strong, loving bond with our dogs, we need to be in sympathy and in harmony with them. This enables us to see the world through their eyes more easily and to understand why dogs are the way they are and why they do what they do.

To make this book easier to read, I have generally referred to dogs as "he," so please substitute "she" if your dog is a female. I have used the real names of the dogs who live, or have lived, with me, but in order to protect client confidentiality I have changed the names of the dogs and owners whose case histories are in this book.

Best friend, companion, helper, and bestower of unlimited love and devotion—this heartbeat drumming at your feet, clothed in fur, is all of these and more. I hope that you enjoy this journey and that every step leads you deeper into understanding, respecting, and treasuring the dogs who share your life.

I

Listening to the Heartbeat

Chapter One

Your Dog's Mind

Skye, my Deerhound-Greyhound Lurcher, stands in front of the wooden shelf where his favorite ball and toys are kept. Although he has some toys left out for anytime use, the ones on the shelf are special playtime rewards, and Skye is hoping that I'll take a break from writing and play ball with him.

His body posture is alert and upright: head high, ears pricked, eyes bright and inquiring. He looks directly at me for a moment, making sure he has my attention, then turns his head to stare at the ball as though willing it to come to life and bounce off the shelf. His gaze returns to me, then the ball, repeating the sequence several times. Skye's intentions are crystal clear, and I was about to take a break anyway.

"Time for a game, Skye?" I ask. Immediately he does a little jump, half-spinning in the air with delight, tail wagging in circles, before sitting and waiting while I get the ball. It's playtime!

Skye wasn't taught how to ask for an out-of-reach toy. He figured out for himself that catching my eye and then focusing on the object he wants will bring results. He's learned that if he points his head, as we would point a finger, my eyes will follow his gaze and I'll get the message. I can't always stop what I'm doing, and on those occasions a quiet "Not now, Skye" will be met with a disappointed but accepting glance, and he'll find something else to do or go to his bed for a nap.

Dogs have their own unique form of intelligence, and this has been put to good use in their relationships with us over many thousands of years. A major element in their long-term survival as a species is that they have learned how to "read" and understand us, how to communicate with us, and how to figure out ways of getting their needs met and serving their interests. Yet every dog is different. Some breeds, such as Collies, are credited as

3

being more intelligent than others, but the ability of all dogs to think, assess, figure things out, and make life easier for themselves is dependent on genetics and on early experiences and their responses to these.

HOW DOES YOUR DOG'S MIND WORK?

Dogs gain an understanding of the world through using all of their senses, and your dog's thinking processes are very powerfully linked with associations, both positive and negative. If a place, person, or experience has been pleasant in the past, the memory of this is retained and your dog will be eager to repeat the experience. If an experience has caused fear, anxiety, or pain, your dog will do his best to avoid that in future.

If you give a treat and praise to your dog when he sits on command, he'll learn to sit for you every time you ask. He's also very likely to go into a sit position without being asked, in the hope that you'll reward him! Conversely, if your dog has had an unpleasant experience, he's likely to want to avoid that experience in the future. During a visit to the veterinary surgeon for Skye's routine checkup, I watched a small lady trying to haul a large long-haired German Shepherd into the clinic from the waiting room. The dog tucked his tail between his legs, dug his heels in, and whimpered pitifully. Nothing would have induced him to go any further because his last visit had created so much fear in his mind, and he was way too large for his owner to carry him through. Fortunately the vet understood and came through to check him over in the waiting room instead of forcing him to go further, but this poor dog was going to need help to overcome his terror of that place.

The dog's powers of reasoning and deduction are less acute than those of wild wolves, who have extremely well-developed problem-solving skills. Partly this is due to dogs' smaller skulls and brains and the different ways in which they are hardwired (remember from the introduction that a dog is a very different creature to a wolf), and partly it is because dogs have evolved alongside us for millennia and tend to look to us for instructions or answers. The intelligence of dogs has been assessed through a great many studies in recent years, and taking the findings too literally by thinking of them as humans in fur coats is doing a great injustice to dogs.

Studies have shown that dogs understand words that fit into the vocabulary of a two- to three-year-old child. Because of this, it can be tempting to consider dogs as having the intelligence of human toddlers and to treat them as if they were children. However, we humans can't sniff out cancer cells in a urine sample or follow a trail for miles or find a person buried deep beneath snow after an avalanche. The intelligence and abilities of dogs are unique to that species and are therefore not subject to simple comparisons with those of other species. A service dog guiding his charge across busy roads or helping with household tasks learns to use his innate intelligence in very specific ways through training that begins at a very early age.

MEMORY AND COGNITION

The short-term memory of your dog is about thirty seconds. After sixty seconds this fades significantly. It relates to things that make no real emotional impact on the dog. For instance, you've been out for much longer than you planned, and you come home to a puddle on the floor and a dog who's delighted to see you. When he realizes that you're calling attention to the puddle, and you're far from pleased, he displays the body language that we tend to associate with guilt or embarrassment—his tail droops, he lowers his body, and he may either move away from you or approach you in an ingratiating manner. What's happening is that, although your dog has no memory of creating the puddle and doesn't associate his earlier "accident" with your displeasure, he's responding to your obvious annoyance and is trying to appease you.

Because your dog's short-term memory is brief, it's vital to show him that his behavior has your approval (or disapproval) while he's actually engaging in that behavior or within thirty seconds of it occurring. This is immensely useful during training. If he receives an immediate reward in the form of your attention, a treat, or a game, he'll choose to repeat the behavior that brought about a reward. In behavior terms this is called "positive reinforcement," and the conditioning (the rewiring of his thought processes) that takes place becomes a deep-rooted habit. Once this occurs your dog will repeat the behavior you're asking for in exchange for praise or acknowledgment instead of food rewards.

Dogs also have long-term memories that can last a lifetime, and these are created through powerful experiences, emotions, or attachments. Once your dog has buried a bone in your back garden, he's unlikely to forget where it is, even a long time afterward. If a place, person, or experience has become associated with fear, anything similar will act as a trigger to the fearful emotion and your dog will respond. This can be dealt with through changing the dog's feelings in the presence of that particular trigger.

Sparky, a young Staffordshire Bull Terrier, was attacked in the park by a black Labrador. From that day on he developed an extreme fear of all black dogs and would try to run away whenever he saw one. If he was on the leash and a black dog approached him, his "flight reflex" was hampered and so he would react by snapping and snarling in an attempt to warn the other dog off. This meant that walk times were very stressful for Sparky and his owner. The solution was to show Sparky that he could feel safe while out with his owner and to gradually accustom him to the presence of black dogs as a source of pleasure instead of pain. This was accomplished by initially turning and walking in the opposite direction when a black dog was around, so that Sparky could gain confidence in his owner's ability to protect him. When his body language showed that he was more relaxed, his owner offered him small pieces of cooked chicken whenever she saw a black dog in the distance, and Sparky's focus on this helped him to associate the presence of black dogs with a special reward. Eventually, through patience and plenty of positive reinforcement, he learned to accept the presence of black dogs and even to walk beside them without responding fearfully.

Long-term memory is revealed through powerful positive emotions, too. A dog who has been through a lengthy separation from his owner, or a person who has been kind to him in the past, will respond ecstatically when they are reunited. Videos of servicemen and servicewomen returning home from overseas to a joyful greeting from their dogs receive a great many hits on YouTube because the sight of these reunions is truly heartwarming and uplifting. The garden of a canine friend is likely to be acknowledged by a pause, a peek, and a sniff as you pass by with your dog, and the same is true if your dog has seen a cat in that garden in the past. And places where food has been offered are rarely forgotten!

Through memory and cognition, dogs understand which experiences are likely to be pleasant or unpleasant. They also learn what is safe and acceptable, and how much they can get away with. A puppy may find that he can jump all over an older dog and a game will result. However, if the older dog is resting, and growls a warning upon being jumped on, the puppy soon learns that playtime is welcomed while his companion is awake and alert, but that it's best to let sleeping dogs lie.

LEARNING

Dogs are fast learners, given the right environment and treatment. You will find out about the crucial importance of the first weeks of life in the section "In the Beginning" later in this chapter and discover why your dog's known background is so important. Like us, dogs learn through experience. If a behavior brings about a reward, that behavior will be learned from and repeated. The reward may be attention, food, the acquisition of a chosen resource, or being left in peace.

Dogs of any age soon learn that praise, affection, a game, and possibly also a food reward are pleasurable and are well worth striving to achieve, whereas being briefly ignored or excluded is unsettling and best avoided.

This, coupled with an innate desire to please (after all, humans are the source of food, shelter, and affection!), makes training using rewards very easy to accomplish.

What you perceive as rewarding, and what your dog sees as rewarding, may backfire on you if you inadvertently create a reward for undesirable behaviors. If your dog barks at people passing by and you tell him to be quiet, you are rewarding him with your attention and he'll carry on barking. He'll even think that you're joining in and encouraging him if his barking reaches a level where you have to shout at him to make yourself heard. If he pulls hard on the leash and you're dragged along behind him with the soles of your shoes burning rubber along the sidewalk, in his mind he is getting to where he wants to go and fast, so he understands that it's well worth getting into a habit of pulling like a steam train every time you take him out. If he growls at a visitor and that person instantly moves away, your dog's reward is getting the outcome he aimed for—that of distance from an intruder—so he assumes that growling will always achieve the desired result. Your responses and reactions, and those of other people, to your dog's behaviors determine whether or not these will continue. Cooperation and an easier, more pleasant life for both of you are achieved through understanding which reward your dog is gaining, from his perspective, and deciding how to redirect this behavior into actions that bring about mutual enjoyment and pleasure.

Your dog's emotional and mental states affect his ability to learn. The most effective time to teach your dog something new is when he's happy and relaxed, as this makes his mind more receptive to fresh inputs and helps him to remember what he's learned so that he can repeat it in future. A tense, stressed dog can't open up to learning something new because his anxiety creates a mental block. This is the same for people, too—when you're feeling under pressure, you're likely to absorb far less information than when you're feeling at ease.

Because stress inhibits the ability to learn, using "dominance methods" to train your dog is counterproductive. Fear and intimidation cause dogs to go into a state of shock and to mentally "shut down." Initially they may seem more obedient because the undesirable behavior appears to be reduced or stopped, but in the long term these methods cause a great deal of harm because the dog loses all trust in his owner and soon either redirects that behavior into another unwanted behavior or stops using the warning signals that had shown his owner that he was about to react. The trainers who use "dominance methods" tend to only show the immediate result rather than how the dog is behaving a few weeks later. When you use the positive Sympatico approach, it may initially take a little longer before you see the results (though often these can be immediate), but the effects are long-lasting.

COGNITIVE MAPS

We humans rely primarily on our visual sense in order to understand the world around us. Dogs' senses of smell and hearing (and, with Sighthounds, their vision) are far superior to ours, and they use all of their senses to create cognitive landscapes that describe their environment and help them to find their way in the future. Smell is the most important sense to your dog, and the mental map that is conjured up through the seemingly simple act of sniffing is vibrant beyond our imagination. Your nose contains around six million sensory receptors that allow you to create olfactory experiences and memories. Dog noses contain between two hundred million and three hundred million scent receptors, depending on the breed of dog, so their world contains a wealth of olfactory stimulation.

On your daily walks you'll most likely pass a favored sniffing area: a tree or a lamppost that the local dogs like to use as a public message board. Let's say it's a tree. Your route will be remembered through what you see along the way, and you'll follow the landmarks that you recognize. On the way there may be a bush of sweet-smelling flowers that adds enjoyment to your walk, but generally you'll be following the visual cues. Your dog, of course, is closer to the ground than you are, so the sights he sees are very different. The scents that he draws in with each breath paint images in his mind that provide masses of mental and emotional stimulation and that give him a plethora of information.

That tree that your dog likes to stop at, and most likely urinate by or against, will smell of bark, of rotting and growing matter, of insect trails, of traces of pollen left by the footprints of visiting bees, of the squirrel who ran up the trunk just before you arrived there, of moisture from the morning dew or last night's rainfall, and of the scents left by every dog who has passed by. The urine scents left behind will tell your dog how big or small these fellow visitors are, their general state of health, whether they are in season—and that's only a small portion of the information he'll be gleaning from nosing around!

When you walk your dog, it can be tempting to (literally) walk—to keep on moving. For we humans, walks are synonymous with exercise, whether this is a slow stroll or a bracing power walk. Allowing your dog to pause for plenty of good sniffs around will expand his mental, as well as physical, horizons. In the wild, dogs don't take themselves off for an hour-long walk twice daily, just for the exercise. They walk to search for food and will spend most of the time in between hunting simply smelling what's happening around them and resting. Thirty minutes of walking and thirty minutes of ambling around sniffing will result in a happy, well-stimulated dog, whereas a power walk with no sniffing time will leave him feeling less tired, more wound up, and rather unsatisfied. He needs the opportunity to fully explore his surroundings and to build up his cognitive maps and make new discoveries about his exercise route.

OBSERVATION AND DEDUCTION

Dogs tend to be more accurate anthropologists than our fellow humans because they observe us closely and understand signals of which we may not even be aware. The sense of smell, described in the previous section, is crucial to your dog's understanding of his environment and his mental well-being. Each of us has a unique personal scent, and this subtly changes when we experience strong emotions such as fear or anxiety. Our body language changes, too. Stress makes us tense up. Shoulders rise or hunch over and the stomach muscles tighten. Another person may not notice, but your dog most certainly does, and he'll immediately respond to what you are feeling.

You will find out more about your dog's visual capabilities in chapter 2, "Instincts and Senses." These are brought into play, along with his senses of smell and hearing, in order to develop opinions about his world and to ascertain whether this seems threatening or pleasurable. Like us, dogs learn through observation and deduction, and there are negative and positive learning experiences. The neighbor's cat may be a source of fascination to your dog, but if he is scratched when he goes to investigate, he will view cats as a source of pain in the future. Your dog may have learned that greeting you at the door with a wagging tail will bring a smile and a show of affection from you. He will recognize that a frowning human is best avoided because past experience may have taught him that a person in a state of tension or irritation will either ignore him or react in an unfriendly manner.

Your dog's experiences, and his observations, determine his behavior. Dogs seek out the easiest route to achieving the goal of the moment, so they take note of, and act on, opportunities that will enable them to feel rewarded.

IN THE BEGINNING

Your dog's breed, heritage, genetics, environment, and early experiences have a significant impact on his or her mind and behavior, so the more information you have about your dog's past, the easier it is to understand how his mind works and how he is likely to respond to different stimuli.

The early environment and experiences of your dog shape his mind and personality. In recent years there has been an outcry against one of the worst exploitations—that of "puppy farming." This is not only cruel, but also leads to all manner of mental, emotional, and physical diseases for the unfortunate dogs who have been bred in such an unhealthy environment. Puppy farms have largely sprung through a desire for particular breeds that happen to come into fashion, and there are few worse places for a dog's life to start or end. Breeding bitches are kept caged in appalling conditions on unhealthy diets; puppies are removed from the mother too early and are not given the basics of care, attention, and socialization that they need in order to lead normal lives. The puppies, when sold to unsuspecting owners, often have health issues that were not obviously apparent in the glow that people feel when acquiring a cute new puppy, and many of these dogs live tragically short lives. Behavior issues are rife because the dog has not had the right start in life and so is unable to cope with the experiences that come his way.

In contrast, the most desirable early environment is one of kindness, comfort, a healthy diet, good medical care, and mental and physical stimulation. These puppies spend their first weeks living with the mother in the breeder's home. They have plenty of opportunity for rough-and-tumble with their littermates, and the breeders and other people who enter the home handle them gently and frequently. This teaches them to socialize with other dogs and with people, and they learn healthy social skills as a result. Playtime with siblings helps to develop their minds and bodies and teaches important lessons such as bite inhibition. If a puppy gets overexcited and nips too hard, his sibling will squeal loudly and walk away. Therefore he soon learns that the game is over if he gets too rough, and he will remember this in his encounters with humans as well as other dogs. Cuddles from and play with the people in his environment teach him that humans are friendly creatures whom he can trust and with whom he can bond. When it is time for him to move to his new home, he will already be prepared for a happy future life.

With rescue dogs, where the background is unknown, we can only make guesses through observing their behavior. A dog who had a good start in life will be more trusting and more open to new experiences than a dog who has experienced neglect or cruelty. Trust can be developed, as you will see through Jack's case history at the end of this chapter, but it takes time, patience, and dedication when a dog has suffered abuse or cruelty.

BREED, HERITAGE, AND GENETICS

Purebred dogs were originally designed for a specific purpose. For instance, Collies were bred to herd sheep. German Shepherds were bred to guard flocks and people. Huskies were bred to pull sledges carrying heavy loads. Sighthounds (Greyhounds, Salukis, Borzois, Scottish Deerhounds, Irish Wolfhounds, Lurchers) were bred for hunting. The breed of your dog tells you a great deal about his basic nature and his thinking processes and therefore informs his behavior. This is most strongly noticed when a dog has come from "working stock," where his parents and their ancestors were actively used for the purpose they were born to, but all dogs carry within them the genetic blueprints of their breed—or breeds, for mixed-breed dogs.

When a dog has been bred for a specific task and isn't given the opportunity to fulfill this, he will redirect his energy into behaviors that are considered undesirable. A Collie, for instance, may redirect his herding impulse into nipping the heels of his human family in order to get them to move into a close group. A Greyhound, who was born to run fast and hunt down small furry animals, may pose a threat to any small furries in his environment if he is not carefully retrained. These actions are instinctual because they were effectively hardwired into the dog's brain many generations previously.

It's vital to understand as much about your dog's background as possible. The characteristics of his breed, or mixture of breeds, and his experiences during the first few weeks of life shape his perception of the world and go a long way toward determining the characteristics that he will display as he grows older. With rescue dogs, often very little (if anything) is known of the dog's past, so an assessment of the breed or likely breed mix, combined with observing how he responds to different stimuli, gives strong indications of how he is likely to think and behave and helps make decisions about what, if anything, needs to be done in order to rehabilitate him.

PERSONALITY TYPES

Every dog has a distinct personality. There are happy-go-lucky dogs who take a positive view of life; shy dogs who hang back nervously when faced with the unfamiliar; energetic dogs who are constantly looking for something to do; couch potatoes who would much rather have a nap than a sprint around the garden; sociable dogs who thrive in company; madcap dogs; confident dogs; serious dogs; protective dogs; fun-loving dogs; dogs who'll do anything for attention; and dogs who like their own quiet space. Each of these will be either an introvert or an extrovert in their approach, though there may be some overlap in different situations. Some dogs are introverted with people yet extroverted with other dogs, and vice versa.

Introverted dogs are easily overwhelmed and find too much stimulation or excitement hard to cope with. They tend to hang back, rather than push forward, in social situations and prefer a quiet space where they can watch from a distance or rest undisturbed. Introverted dogs are rarely competitive, as they'd rather have a quiet life. They dislike having attention focused on them and excesses of fussing or petting and may be shy with strangers. All dogs need routine, but introverted dogs particularly need this in order to feel safe and secure, as disruptions to their usual routine can make them anxious and stressed. They are best suited to living with calm, quiet owners and can be gently eased out of their shells through gentle coaxing and rewards.

Extroverted dogs are the "party-goers" and thoroughly enjoy being in the center of whatever is going on. They're sociable and are at the forefront in greeting visitors. The more company there is the better, in their minds. Extroverts love to play and will often initiate this. If ignored, they'll figure out games of their own and may get up to mischief. Extrovert dogs are more demanding than introvert dogs because they want to be engaged for more of the time and they thrive on positive new experiences. Extroverts need routine, as do all dogs, but they're flexible if their routines are disrupted and may even welcome the change. They are more likely to need firm boundaries than introverts because their exuberance can make them overstimulated and harder to calm down. They are best suited to living with active, sociable owners, as they could become bored and destructive if they are left too much to their own devices.

QUESTIONNAIRE: YOUR DOG'S MIND

Write down your answers to these questions, and then think about what these tell you about your dog's mind. If you live in a family situation with your dog, it can be fun for everyone to answer the questions and then compare notes. You may find that different family members have different perspectives!

- What was your first impression of your dog when you met?
- In which ways do you think the experiences in your dog's early life affect his behavior now?
- Would you assess your dog as an introvert or extrovert?
- Does this assessment apply to your dog's behavior with other dogs as well as with people, or is there a marked difference?
- Does your dog behave differently with people he knows well compared to how he is with strangers?
- What do you think is your dog's experience of a walk?
- Is there anything that your dog especially enjoys? Why do you think this is?

CASE HISTORY: JACK

Jack, a beautiful black Greyhound, was three years old when I was called in to work with him. He had been abandoned and was found half-starved and tethered to a tree by one of his hind legs. He had struggled so desperately to get free that the rope that held him captive had cut through to the bone. When he was rescued and put into foster care, he was extremely traumatized and had lost all trust in people. He was fearful and aggressive, which wasn't surprising as his experiences to date had clearly included horrifying cruelty.

Fortunately for Jack, his wonderfully compassionate foster carers were willing to patiently work to earn his trust, in the hope that he could eventually be happily rehomed. This was a slow process, and at times it seemed that he took three steps forward and one step back. Jack's physical wounds gradually healed, but his mental scars ran deep, and several times his fosterers phoned me, deeply distressed at what he must be going through.

While awake, Jack learned that people could be kind instead of cruel. A blossoming of trust took place with his fosterers, and that slowly grew until he was utterly devoted to them. At first he was antagonistic toward their other dogs, but, with patient handling and plenty of positive reinforcement for friendly behavior, they all became friends.

When asleep, though, Jack's terrible past haunted him in the form of nightmares and night terrors. He would snarl, growl, and snap in his sleep, and his fosterers needed to ensure that neither they nor their dogs were anywhere near his bed while he was resting. At times he seemed to wake from a nightmare but didn't know where he was or who they were until he fully surfaced, and then he would look around in confusion and go to his fosterers to be comforted.

Unstinting patience and understanding paid off. After several months Jack was unrecognizable in contrast to the terrified dog who had suffered so much. His nightmares eased and then faded away altogether, and he bonded so strongly with his fosterers and their dogs that they decided to adopt him. They went on to foster other dogs, and Jack's newly gained confidence enabled him to accept and mentor new temporary members of his social group.

Chapter Two

Instincts and Senses

Stella and Joe, two Labrador crossbreeds, give great cuddles. During my visits to them they rub against me in greeting, overlaying the scent of my dogs with their own. Joe always lies with his head in my lap, pushing his nose into my hand to ask for a stroke when he thinks I've forgotten him. As soon as I arrive home, a canine ritual takes place. Skye, Shep, and whichever other dog I'm currently taking care of engage in discovering where I've been, with whom, and what took place there.

The aperitif sniffing takes the form of short bursts, scattered around all the areas they can reach. Then it intensifies into a main course as they further explore Stella's and Joe's scents by burying their noses against my lap, my arms and hands, my legs. When they're done collecting information, they each give a blowing exhalation, almost a sneeze, as if to say, "Okay, we've figured out exactly what you've been up to!" and wait for the "welcome home" treat that they know will come.

Your dog's instincts and senses are hardwired into him and have developed over millennia for specific purposes, in order to increase his chances of survival and to explore and make sense of his surroundings. We humans have further developed certain instincts and related abilities in different breeds through selective breeding. Instincts and senses work in tandem. For instance, the Sighthound's instinct to chase and catch small furry animals is activated by the sight of something fast-moving, even by a falling leaf or a bird fluttering into the air, and this inherent trait has been further honed, through breeding, so that they could be used as hunting companions and, in the case of Greyhounds, for racing.

PREDATORY INSTINCT

Dogs are natural predators. They were designed to track and kill prey as their sole means of survival. It may seem strange to think of the loving companion dozing at your feet as a predator, and it can be easy to deny this through our desire to humanize our dogs, yet this is his essential nature.

The prey drive has been modified through breeding so that dogs can help us with specific tasks. Collies manipulate the movements of flocks of sheep through their trainers' careful control of their prey drive—without that training, their instincts would lead them to kill the sheep that they are employed to protect. During herding they stalk the sheep, keeping their bodies low to the ground in the classic predator posture; they use the renowned "Collie eye" by staring intimidatingly; they nip at heels if a sheep breaks away from the flock; and, if necessary, they use their voices as yet another means of control. The prey drive of sporting dog breeds is redirected through training them to flush out birds and then, with a "soft mouth," retrieve those that have fallen.

Every dog you meet, no matter how domesticated, is a predator at heart. His senses all come into play when his predator instinct is jump-started, and you can see this occur during games with you and rough-and-tumbles with other dogs. If you watch puppies playing together, they will feint, jump, pounce, and run toward and away from each other, honing their hunting skills. Their sharp needle teeth will be used, unless their playmate squeals to say, "Enough!" They will tug, growling, on toys or pieces of rope that, in their minds, play the role of prey. They are in the process of developing their inbuilt instincts.

SOCIAL INSTINCT

Dogs are social creatures by nature. This is rooted in the simple matter of safety in numbers in the wild, and it increases the chances of success when hunting. A group of dogs can work together more effectively than a lone dog, and this improves the survival odds for each of them.

Our domesticated dogs retain that need for social interaction, even though we provide them with food and shelter. Their survival is dependent on our care, and the number of starving pet dogs found straying is testimony to the fact that their ability to adequately provide for themselves has decreased through long-term domestication.

Dominance theory takes the view that dogs perceive us as members of their pack and that we need to assert ourselves as "alphas" and take steps to ensure that we hold that position. Yet dogs understand that we are not dogs. We don't look like dogs or smell like dogs. We exhibit human, not dog, behaviors. To be with a person who is trying to act like a dog (and, in the case of dominance theory, trying to act like a captive wolf) must create a great deal of confusion! Dogs see us as members of their social group. They bond with us because it is natural and instinctive for them to form bonds and because they have evolved beside us for many thousands of years. Dogs may also bond with other nonhuman members of our households, such as cats, and their social relationships with those animals will be different again to their social interactions with fellow dogs.

The Sympatico method recognizes the special nature of human-canine bonds and bases the relationship on affection and mutual respect for the differences between our species. Through understanding that dogs are social creatures, as are humans, we can take steps to establish and develop the trust that is essential to happy, enduring, successful relationships.

SOCIAL SKILLS

Dogs use a variety of behaviors in order to get along with their canine and human group members. You will find out more about how dogs communicate in chapter 3, "Body Language and Communication," so in this section we'll focus on how they convey their intentions in social interactions with other dogs.

Littermates use play in order to develop their social and predatory skills. Through these games, which are also serious business to them, they learn which behaviors are acceptable and which lead to unwanted conflict or to temporary banishment. Ultimately, dogs prefer not to engage in conflict because this could weaken them if they are injured, and their instinct to survive cautions them to be wary. Behaviors such as squealing when being nipped hard and then walking away have the effect of teaching a playmate to calm down. Puppies have no need for personal space. They engage in constant physical contact, clambering over each other and sleeping in a muddle of entangled bodies.

When puppies meet a new dog, they tend to dive straight into exuberant introductions. With more mature dogs, there is a ritualized process of introduction. Butt-sniffing is the best greeting, as far as a dog is concerned—this is considered polite behavior to dogs, though not to us. The scents that emanate from the rear end and genitals carry a great deal of information, and these are far more revelatory to dogs than an in-depth conversation between two humans meeting for the first time would be. The rear-on approach is also much better manners, in a dog's eyes, than our head-on greeting because immediate face-to-face positioning is a signal that could lead to a challenge or conflict. Two dogs eyeballing each other is a sign to move them apart, whereas as humans, we make connections and assessments by looking into the eyes and tend to distrust people who avoid eye contact.

When dogs gravitate from the rear end to the head, they avoid staring and will turn their heads slightly away to show that their intentions are friendly. One may lick the mouth or face of the other. This is a conciliatory gesture that stems from puppyhood, when they licked the mother's face to solicit food. This says, "I'm friendly, and I acknowledge you."

The position of the body and tail shows a dog's intentions during social interactions, too. Upright posture (standing tall) and a high tail make a dog seem bigger, and the scent is much more immediately apparent, even before butt-sniffing commences. A low body posture or tucked-in tail indicates anxiety, lack of confidence, or fear. A tail that wags slowly from side to side can be a signal to back off or can mean the dog is uncertain of his welcome, depending on other signals he is giving, while an energetically wagging tail and rear end show pleasure.

When dogs are comfortable with each other and want to play, the "play bow" is performed. The front legs are stretched downward while the rump goes up in the air, rather like a yoga position (dogs will often stretch like this on waking, too). This signals a game of chase and tag and is a beautiful sight.

You can easily see how your dog uses all of his senses during social interactions. He sniffs out his companion and uses his nose to get close enough to touch and lick, observes him to check out body language, and listens for any vocal signals such as an excited yip or a warning growl. These senses—smell, sight, touch, hearing, and taste—are vital tools that keep him safe, allow him to understand his environment, and provide immense pleasure. A dog whose nose is buried deep in a patch of grass is experiencing all the delight of a connoisseur inhaling the bouquet of a fine wine.

SMELL

It's early on a February morning. We've had snow for several days, and a thick frost overnight has left the air sharp and fresh. The ground crunches underfoot. Skye stands motionless in the garden, his muzzle extended, flanks quivering, absorbing and processing the scents drifting by. All I can smell is the tanginess of cold air, with undertones of rosemary and sage that Skye released when he brushed past my herb garden. I watch him, guessing at which scent molecules have drifted through and caught his attention. Most likely it's a mixture of the deer in the woods behind the garden, squirrels, badgers, the rank attraction of the fox who calls close by each night, and the scent of the neighboring dogs whose path to the woods takes them past our home. Lately a favored sniffing spot has been all around the pussy willow tree, which we now call the food tree because I hang morsels for the birds from its branches. Skye always hopes that birds may drop crumbs that he can snack on, and sometimes they do.

When your dog catches the tantalizing whiff of a scent, his nostrils quiver and he'll position his nose close to, but not touching, the object of his attention. He exhales to displace air that's already in the nose and to blow the scent upward so that it becomes more intense as he inhales. His breath comes in short puffs, and you'll see his flanks quivering rapidly. The scent molecules he's inhaling travel through the nasal tissues, which are covered in between two hundred million and three hundred million receptor sites, depending on his breed. This is fifty times more than our paltry six million scent receptors, so the information he receives is vast in comparison. Once the signals from the receptor sites reach his brain, the scent molecules are experienced as a smell and are identified.

Positioned above the roof of the mouth, along the floor of the nose, is the vomeronasal organ. This is covered in tiny hairs that transport the scent molecules along their route directly to the brain. Your dog's nose is moist for a reason, thanks to the vomeronasal organ—scent molecules can more easily cling to its damp surface.

Your dog's world is inhabited by scents that are way beyond our sphere of reference. Just as a dolphin or bat uses sonar or echolocation to create images of the environment, your dog inhabits a realm that is abundantly pictured through scents. Everything has an olfactory signature, including you.

We each carry a unique scent that identifies us to our dogs. Even if you wear perfume or deodorant or spent the night in a smoky room, your dog will nose out that it's you beneath those other aromas. When you return after leaving him at home, he knows where you've been and who you've been with, if it's a person he has met before. He can smell the molecules of food that clung to you as you walked through the restaurant you visited, traces of the wine you drank or the meal you ate. He'll want to investigate the scent of the dog or cat you stopped to stroke. And he'll sniff out your innermost feelings.

The reasons for our emotions are often a mystery to dogs, but fear, sadness, anxiety, grief, and intense pleasure subtly change your olfactory signature, and your dog is likely to respond to these changes. When you're afraid, your dog will respond by cringing, removing himself, or acting protectively. When you're celebrating wonderful news, your dog's tail will be wagging. He has a more acute sense of who is trustworthy and whether someone's intentions toward you are good because he can sniff out and see tension, whereas we may take people more at face value. His highly developed senses enable him to hear the visitor before your doorbell rings and to catch a whiff of your scent before you arrive home—the prelude to stationing himself ready to greet you.

TASTE

The senses of smell and taste are interconnected. If something smells disgusting, you're unlikely to want to eat it, and if it smells good, it gets your mouth watering. As dogs have such a highly developed sense of smell, you may expect their sense of taste to be pretty amazing, too—but humans have six times more taste buds than dogs do, and in dogs these are clustered around the tip of the tongue instead of being more widely distributed, as ours are. Dogs can differentiate between bitter, sweet, salty, and sour, and they tend to prefer salty and sweet to bitter or sour tastes, but they rely primarily on their sense of smell for decisions on whether something will be good to eat.

The thought of putting some substances in our mouths repulses us, but those substances don't spark off the same disgusted reactions in dogs. The putrefying rabbit or the fecal matter of another dog isn't something we consider to be edible, but it may be very appealing to your dog, as Riley's owner found in the case history at the end of this chapter. Because their sense of taste is comparatively weak compared with smell, hearing, and sight, strong-smelling foods are more attractive to dogs. This is why a morsel of something smelly, like sardines, mixed into a meal can help to tempt a reluctant dog to start eating.

VISION

Because our eyes are situated to enable us to see what's in front of us, we have 180 degree vision. Dogs' eyes are set more to the side and give them a visual range of 250 to 270 degrees. They're more attuned to the slightest motion than we are and they see better at dusk and nighttime, but the range of colors they see is lower. This is due to the numbers of cones and rods, the photoreceptor cells in the retina at the back of the eye. Signals from these are sent to the brain and translated into color and contrast.

The cones are sensitive to colors. We have more cones than dogs, and ours enable us to see red, blue, and green wavelengths. Dogs see only blue and green-yellow wavelengths, so although they're not color-blind as was supposed until recently, their color range is narrower than ours. However, our comparative abundance of cones doesn't help us to see in dim light because their function is concerned with color.

The rods are sensitive to changes in light and dark, shape, and movement, and dogs have up to three times more of these in the retina than we do. This gives them superior vision at dusk and night and a more acute perception of the slightest motion. The images translated by the brain take the form of snapshots, freeze-frames, at what is called the "flicker-fusion" rate, and if the movement we see corresponds to our flicker-fusion rate, it is perceived as a coherent moving picture. Images passing in front of our eyes at less speed than our flicker-fusion rate will be seen as a series of jerky still-snapshots. The human flicker-fusion rate is sixty cycles per minute. That of your dog is seventy to eighty cycles per minute.

You may have noticed that your dog's eyes glow strangely in photos where you have used the flash on your camera. This is because of the *tapetum*, a layer of cells in the tissue at the back of the eye. This improves night vision and can show up as a blue, green, orange, or yellow sheen when it reflects light. Sometimes dogs with blue eyes or liver or brown coats have no *tapeta*, or it is smaller, and in these dogs the reflection is dull or nonexistent and their eyes may glow red, as ours do, in flash photos.

Before digital television, our analog receptions had a slower flicker-fusion rate of sixty cycles per minute, so dogs would have seen a series of rapid single frames if they looked at the screen. With "faster" digital television, they can see the moving pictures just as we do and can recognize familiar images on the screen. Some dogs take a keen interest in what's showing, and one of my friend's dogs barks at not just every dog he sees on the screen, but also at cartoon characters of dogs—somehow he has cleverly figured out that these drawn representations are similar enough to "real" dogs to merit a reaction! In the United States there is now a television channel called Dog TV, which is specifically designed for dogs to watch and enjoy while their owners are busy.

More images are relayed to your dog's brain than to yours in every minute. So when something moves, such as the ball you just threw or the squirrel running up a branch, your dog sees the arc of trajectory and the landing point before you do. He's poised to catch before you even realize where it will end up!

HEARING

Your dog's hearing, as with his sense of smell, is far more acute than ours and picks up sounds that are way beyond our range. The highest frequencies that we can hear, if our hearing is extremely good, are up to 20 kilohertz. Your dog can tune into frequencies of up to 45 kilohertz, which we consider to be in the ultrasonic range. He can hear the electric appliances buzzing through the wires in your walls, the delicate sounds of insects and rodents outside, the slight rustle of a leaf as it detaches itself from a tree, and your footsteps approaching your gate after a trip out.

The outer ears, so soft to the touch, are called the pinnae. These vary from breed to breed, from the long, floppy, trailing (and mud-attracting) ears of the Bassett Hound to the sharp, upstanding ears of the Jack Russell Terrier who listens for the ultrasonic squeaking of the rats he was bred to hunt. The long, drooping ears of scent hounds have an extra, nonaural purpose, as they waft scents upward from the ground toward the nose, intensifying them for better tracking.

Like us, dogs have an outer ear, a canal that leads into the middle ear, and an inner ear. The *pinna*, the outer ear, channels sound into the ear canal, which is longer and narrower than ours and takes a ninety-degree angle along the way. The *pinnae* move when a sound catches your dog's attention, allowing that sound easy access to the inner ear. A thin membrane, the tympanic membrane, separates the outer from the middle ear, and your dog's middle ear contains three small bones, a cavity of air called the bulla, and a thin tube called the eustachian tube. The delicate inner ear contains nerves for hearing and balance and connects to the brain.

Your dog's understanding of words is thought to be similar to that of a human two- or three-year-old, but his interpretation of the tones and pitches of your voice enables him to grasp the gist of what you're trying to communicate to him, especially if you use your voice clearly and deliberately. The downward-ending inflection of "We went for a lovely walk" may prompt him to prick up his ears at the word "walk," but the upward-ending inflection of "Shall we go for a walk?" is likely to stimulate a more active response before you've even reached for his leash. Likewise, your tone of voice is softer when you're feeling affection and harsher when you feel irritated or annoyed, and your dog will respond to this.

TOUCH

Have you ever wondered why your dog has facial whiskers? These extremely sensitive stiff hairs are called *tactile vibrissae* and are situated above each eye and on the cheeks, the upper lips, and the chin. Each individual *vibrissa* corresponds to a specific area of the brain. They help your dog to map his surroundings and navigate in dim light and confined environments, and they contribute to his facial expressions. Your dog would have used these to seek out his mother immediately after birth, before his eyes opened.

Dogs are social creatures, and touch is as important to them as it is to us. If you watch two or more dogs who live together, you will notice that they frequently sniff each other, touch noses, and make body contact through play in the form of bumping, rolling, and pouncing. A group of dogs who are meeting socially will use their sense of smell first, and then, as they determine that the other dog is friendly, they will engage in more exuberant physical interactions.

The work of Professor Kerstin Uvnas-Moberg in Sweden has revealed how vital touch is to dogs and humans. Her studies into the effects of the hormone oxytocin in the bonding process between new mothers and their babies have also revealed much about our bonds with our dogs.[1] Blood samples showed that when owners stroked their dogs, both the owner and the dog released bursts of oxytocin—the love hormone.

Stroking your dog is good for your health—and his! The heart rate and blood pressure lowers, and sense of well-being increases. If you feel that your dog is an important family member, if you feel love when you think of, or speak of, your dog, this is because the sense of touch has created a chemical bond that links both of you—and that feeling of intense affection is mutual.

EXERCISE

Sit quietly indoors and focus on all of your senses for a few minutes. What can you hear, see, and smell? How do the chair or sofa beneath you and the clothes you are wearing feel? Does one sense feel more acute than the others? Close your eyes for a minute and identify all the sounds around you.

Now step outside and repeat the exercise. If there are flowers nearby, breathe in their scent. You may identify the fragrance, and you may notice a difference between the scent of the blossom and the leaves. Imagine how this must smell to your dog. If he could speak human, he would describe each creature and insect that had brushed past or alighted, and he could tell you whether the droplets of water, barely visible to you, are from rain or dew. This exercise will open your mind to the extraordinary power of your dog's senses.

THE SIXTH SENSE

Dogs have an uncanny ability to attune to our feelings and are often so profoundly linked to us that they can even predict when we are on our way home when we are many miles away. Biologist Rupert Sheldrake has done a great deal of research into this.[2] Documented tests performed on dogs and their owners showed that dogs often anticipate their owners' arrival and will wait by the door with a wagging tail a few minutes, or even longer, before the car pulls up or the front gate opens.

Often a dog's ability to predict your arrival is due to their acute sense of hearing. We each have recognizable footfalls, and dogs quickly learn to differentiate the sound of your car from that of others. Yet Dr. Sheldrake's experiments have revealed that some dogs show distinct signs of anticipation at the moment that their distant owner makes a decision to go home. Somehow, they are able to "tune in" to the mind of the person to whom they are strongly bonded.

Skye is always waiting by the door when my daughter and I have been out, and for a while I assumed that he simply heard us walking down the path—until I observed something very interesting. About ten minutes before my daughter arrived home, at random times during the day or evening and when she must have been too far away to be heard or scented, Skye would get up, go and look out of the window, and then station himself beside the front door. Sometimes I had no idea of when she would be home, so Skye certainly wasn't picking up signals from me. My daughter told me that his behavior was the same when I had been out and she stayed with him. Skye's time-keeping has been consistently accurate throughout his years with us.

The ability of dogs to know when their owners are about to have a seizure is another of their many special gifts, and service dogs are now trained to warn their owners in advance so that they can make themselves as safe as possible. It's likely that a dog who knows you well can pick up minute changes in your scent and in the electromagnetic field that surrounds you, and this is the signal for him to alert you.

There are several explanations for the more mysterious behavior that dogs exhibit. Rupert Sheldrake coined the term "morphic fields" to explain the invisible bonds that link individuals together, even when geographically they are great distances apart.[3] Quantum physics also tells us that everything is interconnected and that distance makes no difference to these connections. Whatever the reason, dogs have a heightened sensitivity to the signals that we are sending out, whether intentionally, inadvertently, or chemically. Their long association with us as a species, and the intense bonds that they forge with us as individuals, has brought about a unique symbiotic relationship based on mutual affection and trust.

The extraordinary range of sights, smells, and sounds that our dogs experience is beyond our imaginings. If we could inhabit, if only for an hour, the glorious, multifaceted world that is normal for our dogs, we would be awestruck by it.

CASE HISTORY: RILEY

Riley, a mischievous Collie crossbreed, was adopted as a puppy and was quick to learn. He bonded swiftly with his owner and quickly understood the house rules and toilet-training. He usually came when called during their walks and grew into an energetic and loving dog. However, whenever Riley smelled a dead animal or fox scat, he suddenly became deaf to all pleas to steer clear. Rolling in it and eating it were Riley's equivalent to a day out at a luxury spa—nothing was better, in his opinion! Of course, he was always horribly sick afterward, usually waiting until he got home so that his owner had a nauseating time cleaning up. Riley's owner was in the process of resigning herself to on-lead walks only, which seemed a shame as they live in beautiful countryside.

When faced with temptation, dogs will choose whatever leads to the greatest reward. For Riley, the prospect of one of his usual treats, and being put back on the lead, was hardly comparable to the sheer doggy joy of indulging in the delight of something extremely smelly. There was no contest. One not very workable solution was to watch out for signs of dead rabbits and fox excrement (though Riley would smell these long before his owner was likely to see them), and the main challenge was to find something that Riley would find even more rewarding should he go dashing off.

Up to that point Riley's owner had chased him, trying to catch him. Not only was this impossible, because he was faster than her, but it also made Riley think that she was engaging in a fun game—so he just increased his speed and dashed further away.

We put together a plan of action. Instead of running after him, calling him, Riley's owner turned and ran in the opposite direction, arms waving as she called his name excitedly. Riley's Collie instincts prompted him to turn to see what she was doing, and then run after her. As soon as he reached her, he had plenty of praise and the reward of some sausage slices or chunks of cheese. She put him on his leash for a minute, just long enough to move him further in the opposite direction to his olfactory object of delight, and then let him off the leash again, repeating the running, calling, and treats if Riley headed back to the source of interest.

Riley soon learned that his owner calling his name meant a special reward, so his recall, his digestive system, and his owner's peace of mind improved enormously!

Chapter Three

Body Language and Communication

The Irish Setter appears suddenly, running out of the woods toward us. From somewhere behind him I hear his owner calling, but he takes no notice. He stops several feet away, tail high, body tense. Tilly, our little foster Jack Russell Terrier, stands perfectly still, her face averted as though the tree beside her totally absorbs her interest. Skye, however, does a little leap into the air, lands, and then extends his front paws and raises his rear end in a bowing position. The Setter's tension visibly melts away; he lowers his body and head, comes close enough to almost touch noses with Skye, and then retreats to where his owner is negotiating the muddy path.

A great deal of communication occurred during this brief interaction, while the dogs figured each other out and decided how they should proceed. Initially the Irish Setter expected conflict and, through his rigidly upright tail and body posture, indicated that he was prepared to defend what he most likely viewed as his territory. By turning her face away, Tilly gave out an instant message that she wasn't interested in conflict of any kind. Skye's way of dealing with the situation was to invite the unfamiliar dog to play with him. The Setter understood that no challenge was forthcoming and backed down. Most likely he had been nervous and decided that a show of valor would protect him.

The language of dogs is fascinating, and it's easy to interpret when you know how. If a picture paints a thousand words to us, a few muscle movements are just as eloquent to our dogs, and the voice is secondary to the clear messages given by the body. The way your dog carries himself, the position of his ears and tail, his level of muscle tension, the direction of his gaze, and the look in his eyes are all indicators of how he is feeling and can be interpreted very clearly.

BODY TALK

Although we consider ourselves to be primarily vocal, we humans constantly use nonverbal communication in our interactions with other people and with animals. When you're anxious or afraid, your body tenses; your jaw, shoulders, and stomach tighten; you may find that your fists are clenched; and your breathing becomes shallower. Even if you're trying to put on an air of bravado, your body and the higher-pitched tone of your voice will betray you. Those around you will subconsciously pick up on, and respond to, your body language, even if this just gives them the sense that something "isn't right" and makes them feel uncomfortable. And when you're feeling good, this shines out like a beacon through the way you carry yourself. When you are calm and at ease, your body is relaxed and your voice is softer and lower-pitched. As dogs observe us closely, they notice every subtle shift in posture and muscle tone and are attuned to the slightest change of inflection in our voices; we will explore this in more detail in chapter 4: "How Your Dog Reads You." This acute observational ability enables dogs to immediately assess what is going on in the minds of people and other dogs in their immediate environment, and by watching the interactions we can gauge this, too.

Body posture speaks volumes, and your dog's body language reveals how he's feeling, what he's thinking, and how he's about to react. Through careful observation you can preempt his actions even before he starts to move. This is especially useful when you see the first signs of anxiety, fear, or aggression, as you can then take immediate action to defuse the situation or remove your dog from the source of that emotion and can therefore prevent a potentially difficult situation from escalating.

Nervous or Fearful

A nervous, anxious, or frightened dog holds his body and tail low. He appears to droop. His head dips, his whole body sinks slightly, and his tail will slip between his legs if he's very scared. His ears are tucked back tightly, and he looks as if he's trying to make himself smaller as a way of showing that he poses no threat to you or to another dog. Body tension draws him tightly into himself, and he may cringe or tremble. The signals that he's transmitting communicate his anxiety and his unwillingness to enter into any conflict.

When a dog is nervous or scared, approaching him or looking directly at him heightens the emotions he's experiencing, and his behavior is likely to escalate into what is called the "freeze, flight, or fight" reflex. Depending on his temperament, he will either become very still, try to escape, or attack. You can show him that you mean him no harm through using body language that helps to calm him. Standing sideways so that you look smaller and less threatening, averting your face slightly so that you aren't looking into his eyes, or turning your back on him all give out a strong message that will enable him to understand that you're not interested in challenging him. You can also use these signals with dogs who bark or growl at you.

Depressed

A depressed dog shows similar body posture to an anxious dog. It may seem strange to think of dogs as suffering from depression, but this does occur, and it's a fairly common sight for veterinary surgeons. Causes of depression include physical or mental abuse, the loss of a much-loved owner or animal companion (through bereavement or through the dog having to be rehomed), and through any change of circumstances. Other common triggers are a new baby or puppy appearing on the scene and taking the usual attention and affection that previously was given to the dog. Rescue dogs in shelters some-times show distinct signs of depression, noticeable because of their body posture and through a lack of energy, a loss of interest in food, or disinterest in interactions with other dogs and people. Depressed dogs tend to isolate themselves and will hide away. They often avoid eye contact, and their eyes are devoid of that spark of curiosity and interest that we expect to see in the dogs we meet. Lulu, one of my foster dogs, showed all the classic signs of fear and depression.

Lulu was brought into rescue after being used as a racing and then breed-ing Greyhound. When I met her for the first time, her plight brought tears to my eyes. She had been described to me as being totally "shut down" and unresponsive and was cringing and quaking at the back of her kennel, body tucked as tightly as possible, head averted to avoid any risk of eye contact. Lulu had been beaten in the past, and she was terrified of everyone and everything. Coming into the noisy environment of the kennels fuelled her fear even more intensely and contributed further to her depression, and it seemed that she had "given up." No one could approach Lulu without her retreating further, and any chances of finding a forever home for her ap-peared to be very slim indeed.

I sat outside her kennel with my back to her, my body relaxed, speaking very softly and reassuringly occasionally so that she could get accustomed to my voice. After a while I heard the click of claws on concrete and felt soft breath on the back of my neck. Very, very slowly I turned slightly so that my body was angled sideways. This made me seem smaller and less threatening to her, while allowing me to use peripheral vision to observe her. Lulu stayed close to the bars of the cage. In slow-motion movements, whispering that she was now safe, I placed a few treats just inside her kennel. After a moment's hesitation, Lulu delicately took them and stayed close to me. Still in a side-ways position, my face averted, I extended the hand that held the treats so that it was right beside the bars. Lulu, to my delight, pushed her nose through and took the treats and then sniffed my hand. I left my hand there so that she could absorb my scent and carried on talking gently to her while I oh-so-slowly turned to face her, taking more treats from my pocket and placing them on my outstretched hand. Within just a few minutes Lulu was allowing me to gently touch her, and she took a step back only when I carefully opened the kennel door, slipped through, and sat on the floor. Soon she was standing resting against me, then leaning in while I stroked her and spoke to her before slowly rising and slipping on her leash. She followed me willingly to the car for the ride home.

Lulu's rehabilitation took almost three months. She trusted me and quickly grew to trust my daughter, but she removed herself from the room when visitors came and cringed at the sight of strangers during our walks. Patience, the use of calming body language, and gradual calm introductions to new people and experiences paid off, and Lulu was eventually adopted by a caring new owner.

Confident

A confident dog with nothing to fear is a joy to behold. His body is held upright, head high, eyes bright and alert, and he sports an upstanding or slightly raised tail. His ears are upright or loosely relaxed, and he shows no signs of tension. Confident dogs are comfortable in their own skins. They take new experiences, people, and dogs in their stride and approach life with a sense of gusto. I've met many people who confuse "confidence" for "dominance," who make the assumption that a confident dog has a mindset geared toward ruling over his environment. This is false. Dogs should be confident; their natural state is one of keen inquiry and openness.

A confident dog isn't pushy or bullying. He greets life's occurrences with equanimity and has no interest in being domineering. Although confident dogs refrain from competing (why should they compete, when they feel sure that life will treat them well?), in any group of dogs the dog who exudes confidence is one whom the others look to for guidance, and he will display this through his polite treatment of those in his group. Dogs who bully others are, in fact, showing openly that they lack confidence; bullying, in dogs as in people, indicates insecurity.

Happy

When your dog is feeling happy, his body posture is relaxed, his mouth will be open, and his tongue may hang out so that he seems to be smiling. A wagging tail completes the picture. If he's alert and happy (for instance if he's waiting for you to throw the ball he just dropped at your feet), his ears will prick up and he'll look expectantly at you. The same language can be seen when you pick up his leash or mention your intention of taking him for a walk or head toward the place where you keep his treats or toys. He may even perform a little hoppity-skip dance of joy.

You can tell when your dog is boisterously or quietly happy simply by looking at him, and you may see this even when he is asleep. Lucy, one of my Greyhounds, was elderly when she came to live with us, and all she wanted was love, good food, and company during her final few months. Lucy was such a happy soul that she appeared to be constantly smiling, and it would warm my heart to watch her as she lay dreaming beside me because she wagged her tail even in her sleep.

Angry/Aggressive

Standing tall and stiffly to attention; rigid legs and ears; rounded, staring eyes that seem to protrude from the sockets; raised hackles—these are all signs that a dog is about to attack, and they should be taken very, very seriously. Usually warning signals are given before a dog feels compelled to take violent action, and noticing these and acting on them can help to prevent you or another dog from being bitten.

If a dog growls, barks aggressively, or stares hard at you, or if you notice that his body has become tense and his ears have flattened against his head, you can use the body language described in the section on nervous or fearful dogs to indicate that you're not willing to engage in conflict. Turn away and cross your arms, avert your face, and avoid looking directly at him. Take slow breaths, as this helps you to stay calm and the dog will sense your tension or fear. On no account raise your voice to him, as this is likely to provoke an attack; if you must speak, use a quiet, calm tone of voice. Move very slowly away from him, never toward him, as sudden movements or an approach will seem threatening to an angry dog.

There are three main causes for aggression in dogs. Anger is often the result of fear, of feeling threatened, and in these cases attack seems, to the dog, to be the best way of defending himself. Aggression is also caused through owners who treat their dogs harshly, who use dominance methods as a way of keeping control, and many of the aggressive dogs I have worked with have become this way because they felt there was no alternative but to protect themselves from abuse. Aggression can also result when a dog is protecting something that you're trying to remove from him. You'll discover effective, nonconfrontational methods of dealing with what is called "resource guarding" in chapter 10: "Barking, Chewing, Growling, and Other Issues."

Worried or Insecure

The signs of worry and insecurity are similar to those of a nervous dog. The body tenses and lowers, and his head will dip. He may shrink back or try to hide behind you. With most breeds of dogs you can see their eyebrows, the little tuft of *tactile vibrissae* just above the eyes, and these shift into an upward-slanting angle, just as our eyebrows do when we feel worried.

The intentions and emotions of dogs whose eyes are hidden, such as Old English Sheepdogs, are sometimes misinterpreted because dogs rely strongly on the subtle signals given by the eyes, and these can't be seen in breeds whose eyes peek out through a fringe of hair.

When a dog wants to communicate appeasement or reassuring submissiveness, he may perform what is termed a "submissive grin." This is unfortunately often misinterpreted by humans as aggression, because the upper lip curves back to display the top front teeth. However, where the body rises and tenses, the eyes protrude, and the ears lie flat as signals of imminent aggression, the submissive grin is accompanied by low body posture, narrowed eyes, and often sounds such as whining or squeaking.

An insecure or concerned dog gains confidence and reassurance through your calm body language. If you make a fuss and offer profuse sympathy, this will only reinforce his anxiety. Calmly telling him that there's no need to worry and stepping between him and the source of his worry shows him that he can feel safe with you and can relax.

Excited

If you mention a walk or dinner or bring out a toy, your dog's joy and excitement will be apparent in his bright eyes, upright body, and sudden influx of energy. He may leap, jump, or dance in his eagerness to communicate to you that he's delighted about the turn of events.

Being around an excited dog can be fun, but overexcitement and exuberance can easily get out of hand. If you want him to calm down a little, lowering your voice and turning away until all four paws are on the ground will help to reduce his excitement. Of course, if you're in play mode, you're likely to thoroughly enjoy his expressions of delight!

Relaxed

Floppy ears; soft, half-closed eyes; a slightly open mouth; and fluid body posture are all signs of a relaxed dog. Dogs will often expose the most vulnerable areas of their bodies through lying on their backs, legs akimbo, when they're very relaxed.

If you want your dog to relax or to fall asleep, you can bring this about through keeping your voice soft and low and through slowly blinking your eyes. This has a slightly hypnotic effect and your dog is likely to soon be resting at your feet.

STRESS SIGNALS

We humans often consciously or subconsciously mirror the body language of the people we are with, especially if we feel an emotional connection with them. This has the effect of creating a rapport with the other person. If we sense that someone is anxious, we automatically speak more softly and move more slowly. Dogs have their own way of attempting to reduce stress in other dogs and in their human companions.

Nervous or anxious dogs display clear signals that they feel uncomfortable. Although these are often called "calming signals," they are signs that the dog feels stressed and is communicating that he isn't a threat, in the hope that the source of the stress will be removed. When you see your dog giving these signals, you can mirror the pertinent one in order to reassure him that you mean him no harm. However, care should be taken not to overdo this, as otherwise your dog may think that you are also stressed, and this will make him more anxious. He needs to feel secure in your presence.

Moving very slowly, freezing in position, yawning, lowering the body, sitting or lying down, turning the head sideways to avoid eye contact, softening the eyes, blinking, rolling on the back (and urinating, if a dog is extremely worried), nose-licking, turning away to sniff the ground, tail-wagging, play-bowing, stepping in between two dogs who are getting overexcited, and moving in a curve rather than head-on are all signals that are intended to defuse tension and show that your dog wants to be friendly. The stress signals/calming signals are part of your dog's repertoire of polite behavior, and if you watch closely, you will see that he uses these a great deal with you and with other dogs.

You can use some of these, too, if you need to reassure your dog. Although dogs who trust us will gaze lovingly into our eyes, in many cases direct eye contact is considered to be hostile, so averting your eyes slightly makes an unknown dog feel more comfortable. You may have noticed that you give a certain "look" to your dog if you are displeased with him—a hard stare—and that he immediately responds by looking away. His body language is telling you that he's deferring to you. Blinking slowly, turning your face and body away, yawning, and moving in a curve will all tell your dog that he can relax; that there is nothing to fear.

HOW DO DOGS LEARN BODY LANGUAGE?

Your dog's basic body language and communication skills are instinctual and are honed through interaction with the mother, littermates, and the humans in his early environment. A dog who is lacking in these essential skills is likely to be either shunned or attacked by other dogs, so, as dogs are social creatures, they quickly figure out which behaviors and signals are most rewarding and then repeat these. They learn through observation and the direct experience of trial and error.

A dog who has been removed too early from the litter doesn't have the opportunity to develop social skills and an in-depth understanding of canine body language. This can ultimately be dangerous for him, as he may be unable to interpret the intentions of other dogs or may use inappropriate body language that sparks hostility in other dogs.

In their relationships with us, we have a profound effect on their nonverbal displays. Rewards for using particular signals are likely to reinforce those signals, and punishment can cause them to be suppressed. We can use this to our advantage by responding positively to calm body language. Our approval means a great deal to our dogs, so they will continue to use signals that have brought rewards in the form of affection, a game, or food treats. However, dogs who have been punished for showing signs of irritation, discomfort, or anger through growling soon learn that giving a growl leads to pain. In order to avoid this, they may suppress the warning growl and move straight into the bite instead.

Because of the long association between humans and dogs, your dog's brain is hardwired with the ability to observe and act on your body language. He may not understand the reasons for your feelings, but he can pick up the signals that reveal whether you are happy, sad, frightened, angry, or playful. If two people are arguing, the dog in the room will take one of three options to deal with the situation. He may remove himself as far away as possible to escape the conflict; he may try to move in between you, in order to separate you ("splitting up"); or he may growl at or challenge the person he views as attacking the human to whom he is most strongly bonded.

When you are relaxed, he is likely to relax, too, and when you are upset he may try to comfort you through sitting close by or licking your hand or face. Licking is a gesture of appeasement and reassurance, performed to let you know that he is "there" for you.

TALKING DOGS

Dogs use a wide range of sounds in order to communicate, and a research study by Dr. Adam Miklósi at the Eötvös Loránd University in Budapest, Hungary, revealed that dog-savvy humans can correctly interpret the sounds that dogs make, even when recordings of unknown dogs are played to them. [1] Distress, fear, excitement, anger, playfulness, excitement, warnings, and sadness were all correctly pinpointed by a number of dog owners, simply through listening to different types of vocalizing.

Depending on the tone and pitch, a high yip can mean anxiety or excitement. A low whine can signal boredom, anxiety, fear, or pain. A low rumbling growl is a warning, but some dogs will make growling sounds through excitement during play. A high-pitched bark is a call for help or attention, whereas a low bark is a signal to alert others to an intruder. Yelps mean pain or fear.

EXERCISE

Pay attention to what your dog is communicating to you. You can take just a few minutes each day, at different times of the day, to observe him, but you may well find that you become so fascinated by how your dog reveals his emotions that you start to pay much closer attention to him whenever he is in your presence! Ask yourself these questions:

Does your dog have a particular greeting ritual, such as lowering his body, jumping up, licking you, or dancing around?

What does your dog do when you prepare to go for a walk or feed him or instigate a game or get ready to go out without him?

Does your dog greet familiar dogs differently to unfamiliar dogs?

Which vocal signals does he tend to use the most? Think about why he uses these.

CASE HISTORY: CARNIE

Carnie was handed over to us by a local farmer when he was just a puppy. A mixed breed of indeterminate heritage (though I suspected a small sprinkling of Collie in him), he looked like a small, round black bear—a bundle of fluff and playfulness. He curled tightly against me in the car on the way home and, on arrival, decided that my lap was his personal resting place—this continued even when he was way too large to fit on it without half-smothering me!

Carnie had the sweetest nature and threw himself wholeheartedly into games with my children. He was respectful of our elderly dog and our cat, ignored my small flock of chickens and my sons' pet rats, and was the most efficient food thief I've met to date. Nothing was too hot or inaccessible for him, and he perfected the art of silently lying beneath the kitchen table, ready to stealthily pounce and grab the moment my back was turned. Carnie grew up into a beautiful wolf-like black dog with immense character and an unlimited capacity for bestowing affection. We all adored him.

Carnie's greatest talent, besides stealing, was vocalizing. He sang eloquent, full-throated harmonies when I played my guitar. He yipped with glee while chasing my sons around the garden. He growled fearsomely during games of tug, relinquishing the rope instantly if the children pretended to growl back. He knew when we were preparing to go out and leave him at home and would whine plaintively, body low, ears back, and eyes soft with pleading—even though he was fine once left, he was a virtuoso at guilt-tripping. And he "talked" back, cleverly imitating tones of voice and then lolling his tongue as if to laugh and say, "That surprised you, didn't it?"

When Carnie passed away he took a piece of my heart with him, but he left behind an abundance of happy memories that always make me smile. The greatest gift he brought was that of unconditional love, but close behind, in second place, was his extraordinary ability to reveal and express every feeling that he experienced, in such an infectious way that these were communicated to every human within his sphere.

Chapter Four

How Your Dog Reads You

It's a beautiful sunny morning, and I should be doing a number of things. Writing, household tasks, catching up on mail, and tidying the garden are just a few of the items on today's to-do list. The sunshine beckons. It seems a shame to be indoors, and Skye knows exactly what's going through my mind when I briefly look out of the window. He's lying beside me and he seemed to be dozing, but suddenly his head and ears come up and he gazes directly at me, waiting.

The moment I make the decision to go out for a short stroll, before I have moved from the computer or said one word or even glanced in Skye's direction, he's up and dancing, head nodding pointedly toward the hook in the hallway that holds his harness and leash. The walk energizes me for the rest of the morning, and Skye, his senses temporarily satiated by all the scents he's absorbed, sleeps close beside me while I work.

Dogs have what often seems to be an uncanny ability to decipher our thoughts and intentions. Their close attention to us, even when they seem to be dozing, can also teach us a great deal about how revealing our mannerisms are. Creatures of habit by nature, we develop our own little rituals that dogs very quickly come to recognize. When we're about to move from the room or prepare to go out, we may glance toward the door, shift our shoulders back, or stretch a little before getting up. Our faces and bodies display tiny hints of a change of focus, micro-movements that the people around us may not notice. Our body language and tone of voice when we are relaxed, tense, afraid, angry, or feeling affectionate send out signals to our dogs that their human-scanning radar instantly picks up and identifies. This is further compounded through subtle changes in our scent.

This talent for observation and deduction can be put to good use when we train our dogs. Your dog knows when he's done something right because your pleasure is evident to him. You'll most likely praise him, smile, and pat him, and your body will be "open" and relaxed. You may also give him a treat or a toy to further reinforce the desired behavior. If you're displeased, you will most likely frown, turn away, or use a harsher or louder tone of voice than usual. Dogs have an innate desire to please us, partly because this consolidates their continuing membership in our (and their) social group and partly because receiving praise and approval feels good.

TONE OF VOICE

As your dog's hearing is far more acute than yours, he can pick out even slight changes in the tone of your voice. When you're relaxed, your voice is softer and lower-pitched. When you are tense or scared, your internal as well as external muscles tighten, so your voice sounds strained and slightly higher in pitch. Happiness opens the throat, so your voice sounds lighter. If you are angry, you may raise your voice, and the combination of strong emotion and muscle tension makes it sound harsher as well as more strained. When you feel affectionate, your voice takes on a crooning quality, with a softer tone than usual.

You can consciously use your voice as a way of communicating with strange dogs, as well as your own dogs. As many of the rescue dogs I work with have been through immense trauma, I deliberately keep my voice very soft and low when speaking to them. This helps to reassure them, and often very nervous or fearful dogs will then feel safe enough to pay attention and come closer, as with Lulu, whose story is told in chapter 3: "Body Language and Communication." A soft voice helps to engender trust because the tone has a calming effect.

POSTURE

When you consider the differences between the arrangement of our bodies and that of dogs, it seems even more extraordinary that they interpret so much of our body language so accurately. We stand upright on two legs. Our arms are set high, with the hands usually held lower, and we tend to move them a lot. Our delicate belly and heart areas are face-on, rather than underneath. A dog's everyday view of us when we are fully upright, rather than seated, is of our legs, and they have to look up in order to see the top part of our bodies and our faces.

When we feel defensive, we hunch inward and cross our arms. Relaxed, we spread out our bodies, with hands open and fingers unfurled, and we move more fluidly. When we're angry, we tense up as though to spring, our eyes become narrow or grow much wider, and our hands clench to unconsciously form fists. Movements are jerky and exaggerated. Dogs recognize these signs, even when they merely show as slight muscle tension or movements. Our bodies express and translate our emotions.

You can use this understanding of posture to communicate nonverbally with unknown dogs, as well as with your familiar companion. If a strange dogs races full-tilt toward you and you're unsure of his intentions, you can stand sideways, with your arms crossed against your chest and your face and eyes averted, keeping your body relaxed and still. He will immediately understand that you are not interested in conflict and that you are standing your ground in a nonthreatening way. Most dogs, even those who were considering aggression, will slow, then stop, perhaps sniff around your legs for a moment, and then walk away.

When you meet a dog who is nervous, anxious, or scared, you can use body language to reassure him. Take a deep breath and then breathe slowly, as this will help you to feel calmer. This will be immediately transmitted to the dog. Hold yourself upright, but relax your muscles. If you feel any tension in your body, breathe through it so that it melts away. Be still as much as possible, and when you do move, move very slowly. Take care not to stare at him; use your peripheral vision for observing him. Make yourself look smaller, either through a sideways stance or through crouching down or sitting. Make sure your hands are relaxed and open, and let him sniff your hands if he wants to, being careful to avoid the temptation to stroke him until his body language shows that he too is relaxed. As you will see later in this chapter, your hands speak volumes to a dog.

IT'S IN THE EYES

Unfamiliar or nervous dogs try not to engage in eye contact in order to avoid having to deal with a possibly challenging situation, and it's unwise to gaze into a strange dog's eyes unless they are clearly relaxed in your company, as this can be interpreted as a prelude to aggression. However, dogs who know and trust us will often actively seek out eye contact with a human as a way of strengthening the emotional bond. Considering how they avoid this with other dogs, it's remarkable that they have learned that we perceive eye contact as an expression of affection and are willing to set aside their instinctual distaste for this and choose to look deeply into our eyes. The pleasure of a long, loving look from across the room or of a dog resting with his head on your lap, gazing up at you, is one of the most beautiful and heartwarming affirmations of how close our furry friends wish to be to us.

LEFT GAZE BIAS

Dogs are the only creatures, apart from humans, who use what is termed the "left gaze bias" to decipher the emotions of another person. The right side of a person's face is thought to reveal more clues as to a person's emotional state, so we tend to look left, at the right side of someone facing us, to more accurately "read" them.

Professor Daniel Mills, Dr. Kun Guo, Dr. Kerstin Meints, and their team at the University of Lincoln in England have conducted experiments into left gaze bias in dogs.[1] The studies indicate that dogs, like people, use left gaze bias most strongly with human faces, even when photos of these are shown upside-down. Even chimpanzees, the creatures considered to be our closest cousins, don't use left gaze bias.

This desire and ability to figure out our emotional states helps dogs to decide whether it is safe to come close to us, if we are smiling or looking relaxed, or whether they should move further away, if we are frowning, tense, or angry.

HANDS

Humans are creatures of gestures. Our hands and arms move a great deal. We move our hands to make a point while we are talking, we describe arcs in the air with our hands and arms when excited, and we shake a fist or wag or poke a finger when angry. When we want someone to stop talking or doing something we don't like, we hold up our hands, palms outward. We point a finger to draw someone's attention to an object or person of interest. We wave to catch someone's eye, and we wave our hands slightly differently, with accompanying facial expressions, to show disgust or that we wish for more physical distance.

Certain of our hand and arm movements speak volumes to dogs. Putting your hand up, palm out, in the "stop" position tells a dog to immediately cease his behavior. A pointed finger that gives direction is likely to quickly be noticed by your dog, whose eyes will map out the trajectory of your finger so that he can see what you want him to see.

Dogs point too, but (not having fingers) they use their noses. Your dog will know where the treats or favorite toys are kept and may stand and extend his nose toward the storage place in order to let you know that he really would appreciate it if something good came his way. Dogs will also use their noses to point out something interesting to the other dogs in their environment. It's quite a sight when a group of dogs gather around the dog who is pointing at something on the ground, all of them keen to find out exactly what's happening in that spot!

Skye is nervous of spiders since a very large hairy one ran across his face while he was sleeping one night. His yelp of horror was accompanied by an impressive leap into the air, followed by intense sniffing and a nose pointed firmly at the spot on the floor where the spider had landed. He stayed in that position, glancing back and forth pointedly at me, until I caught the offending spider (it was huge!) in a jar and set it free outside. Now, whenever he sees a spider, Skye stands rigid, nose aimed directly at his bête noir, until I catch and liberate it.

A human hand approaching a dog may mean the pleasure of a caress or the pain of a beating. Dogs who have experienced abuse tend to be hand-shy because they expect the worst. Even well-treated dogs may become nervous if a human makes a sudden hand or arm movement toward them or touches them directly on the head. A slow, gentle approach reassures a dog that you come in friendship, especially if you move carefully to initially stroke the body or behind the ears, rather than the top of the head. Some dogs dislike being patted, especially strong pats that must feel to them as if they are being hit.

SMILING

We smile to show pleasure and to reveal that our intentions are friendly. Among our repertoire is the shy, closed-mouth smile; the quick curve of the lips that means amusement; the wry, upward twist when we feel we shouldn't find something funny, but do; and the wide, tooth-revealing grin of delight.

A dog showing his teeth at another dog is a warning to back off, so dogs don't smile at other dogs. But they have learned to communicate joy and a sense of kinship toward us by displaying the irresistible doggy smile—lips parted over the teeth to create a curved mouth. Some dogs manage crescent-moon-shaped closed-lip smiles, too. Only humans are treated to these displays of affection (and, occasionally, ingratiation, if your dog wants to win back your favor after a misdemeanor) because dogs have learned that we smile at them when we are pleased or happy.

Dogs adapt their behavior in order to fit in with us and to strengthen the bonds between themselves and us. That they act in ways that go against their instincts, simply to let us know that they understand the meanings of our facial expressions and wish to communicate their emotions to us, is yet more testimony to the strength of their desire to foster affectionate relationships with us.

WHEN HUMAN BODY LANGUAGE CREATES CONFUSION

Sometimes dogs get it wrong. If we always use the same body language to communicate with dogs as we do with humans, we may give a conflicting impression through our signals. Take the eyes, for instance. The *sclera*, the whites of our eyes, show more when we express surprise, shock, fear, or excitement or when we are really pleased to see someone we know. In dogs the sclera is mostly hidden and usually can only be seen when they are either very afraid or very angry. One of the signs of imminent aggression to a dog is eyes that widen and protrude, with a portion of the sclera showing. Widening your eyes at a dog, especially if you are gazing at him or staring at him, will be read as a sign that you're trying to intimidate him.

Another tendency that we humans have is to physically come very close to those who we consider to be "cute," such as babies, children, young animals—and dogs, especially small or very appealing-looking dogs. This usually takes the form of looming over them, reaching in to touch them (often on the head), or moving to pick them up, all the while raising the pitch of our voices. This attention from a stranger can be unnerving and scary for dogs.

HOW NOT TO APPROACH A DOG

Imagine, for a moment, that you are a dog. A stranger approaches you at speed or suddenly stops right in front of you. (Is she going to attack me? I'm feeling nervous.) The stranger's body looms over, huge and threatening (Oh, no! She is going to attack me—I'm really feeling scared now!) A high-pitched voice squeals out how cute you are. (I'm being warned of danger!) A hand suddenly appears out of the air to land on your head. (Help me, please!) The stranger may pick you up if you are small or lean over to thrust her face into yours if you are larger. She may even kiss you. (She's about to sink her teeth into me!) Her eyes are large and wide as she tells your owner how beautiful you are.

By now you, in your temporary guise of a dog, are terrified and can't understand why your owner isn't protecting you. If you try to escape and cannot, your only recourse may be to utter a warning growl or to snap at the offending hand. The stranger is shocked, not realizing that she has just broken all the rules of doggy good manners by approaching too suddenly and closely and by giving out signals that you interpret as being threatening.

Dogs approach from the rear or in a curve to show their intentions are benevolent. If a dog wants to show another dog that he is not to be messed with, he may invade the other dog's space by looming over, making deliberate eye contact, putting his head over the neck of the other dog, or even by mounting to show that he intends to win if challenged. Knowing this makes it easy to understand why the dog whose body and mind you just briefly inhabited felt so intimidated.

MIRRORING

We mirror the body language of people to whom we feel close or whom we wish to encourage to relax. This helps to facilitate a natural bond by creating an atmosphere of ease and harmony—people feel more "in tune" with those who use similar body language and gestures.

In the interests of research, a behaviorist friend and I did an experiment in mirroring. We tried yawning when our dogs yawned, sighing when they sighed, getting down on the floor to imitate a play-bow—much to our dogs' delight! You can try this yourself. Most likely you'll notice that when you go down on the floor on all fours, your dog becomes playful and dances around you. If you sigh heavily or yawn, your dog soon follows suit.

STRANGE ASSOCIATIONS

Because dogs watch us so closely, they pick up on mannerisms and habits that we are often unaware of having. Sometimes they take advantage of distractions. One complaint I often have from clients is the difficulty of conducting a phone conversation because their dog starts to bark, chew things, ask to go out, or generally makes a nuisance of himself as soon as the phone rings. The dog has learned that the strange one-sided conversation he can hear when his owner talks into a piece of plastic means that he'll be ignored for a while.

Peculiar associations often come about by accident. We live in the countryside, and I always take Skye, and any other dogs staying with us, to meet Amber, my daughter, at the end of the mile-long lane by our home when she returns from college. She sends me a text to say she's on her way, and I answer it and then prepare to leave the house. After a few days I noticed that Skye would leap up and wait by the door every time a text message arrived. He had developed an association between the beeping sound and a walk. A quiet shake of my head became his signal to move away from the door and relax if the message wasn't from Amber.

THE POWER OF THE VOICE

Dogs listen carefully to the tones of our voices and decide how to react depending on what meaning they have interpreted. Even words or phrases that your dog understands as being beneficial to him will be reinterpreted if your tone of voice changes. If you say, "Good dog," in a harsh voice, your dog will act as though you are angry with him. He may lower his body or move away. Croon, "Who's a bad boy?" and his tail may wag because he associates that tone of voice with affection.

You can use your tone of voice alongside your body language in order to communicate effectively with your dog, and you don't need to shout or raise your voice to get him to listen. In fact, if you habitually raise your voice a great deal, he's more likely to ignore you—just as children tend to do— because the volume loses its impact. A soft voice reassures and comforts him. A firm or sharp voice tells him that you are not pleased. Your dog reads your emotional state through a combination of body language, facial expressions, and tones of voice.

EXERCISE

Think about your habits and how your dog responds to the first signs of any habitual behavior on your part. Perhaps you always look for your keys or pick up your cell phone before you go out. Or maybe you stretch before going to prepare a meal or look in the direction of the toys while you think about whether you have time for a game. Your dog's responses can tell you a great deal about the unconscious signals that you give out.

CASE HISTORY: HOW JOHN OVERCAME HIS FEAR OF DOGS

John, who was in most respects a confident, extroverted teenager, confessed that he was terrified of dogs. Whether they were small or large, calm or friendly, he took care to avoid them, even to the extent of crossing the road if an owner and dog were walking toward him. As I had three large dogs living in my home at that time, he would sidle in carefully, flinching even when my ultra-calm old Greyhound, Orla, merely wagged her tail in greeting. John told me that he had been bitten, though not seriously, several times by strange dogs and that even dogs who seemed friendly initially would growl at him.

Observing John's body language around my dogs revealed that he was unintentionally sending out all the wrong signals. He couldn't do anything about the acrid scent of fear that his body was creating, but I pointed out that by changing his body language and the signals he was sending out, he could relax a little and develop a more positive relationship with dogs. He decided to try this, even though he expressed doubts that it would make any difference. "Dogs just don't like me," he said.

What was John doing that antagonized or unsettled dogs? He stared at them in order to literally "keep an eye" on where they were and what they were doing. He placed his (very tall) body rigidly full-frontal, facing them. His breathing was rapid and shallow, which only increased his fear and which consequently intensified the scent of rushing adrenaline. When he couldn't move away from a dog, he put his hand out as though to pat the dog on the head, withdrawing it quickly at any movement from the dog, and he spoke in a very loud voice to try and pretend that he wasn't feeling scared. This combination made approaching dogs feel anxious and insecure.

I suggested that John breathe more slowly and deeply, as this would help to relax him as well as the dogs he encountered. Lowering his voice and speaking softly reassured them that he was friendly. Turning away slightly, with his arms crossed high over his chest or tucked into his sides, would make him seem less intimidating. Using peripheral vision instead of staring directly at the dog meant that he was observing the rules of doggy good manners instead of seeming to want to challenge the dog, and this would defuse tension on both sides. I pointed out that he wasn't obliged to touch or pat dogs who came close—just saying, "Hello," in a quiet voice was a good enough greeting. Any movements he made should be slow and fluid.

We practiced on my dogs first of all. As all of them were friendly and polite, though Skye could get bouncy when excited, this helped to build John's confidence. Within an hour of coming in and out repeatedly, he was walking through the door using this new approach and was feeling very pleased with himself that he could greet my dogs without feeling scared.

Within a few days he was initiating tactile greetings and thoroughly enjoying the interactions, to the extent of engaging in games of ball and really having fun. It was a pleasure to see him so relaxed and to hear him laughing at the dogs' obvious enjoyment of his company.

Away from our home, John practiced focusing on the signals he was giving out to unfamiliar dogs and consciously relaxed each time he felt his body become tense. Several months later he told me that every strange dog he met had been friendly toward him, and (to his surprise) he had discovered a genuine affection for dogs. Of course, the dogs he met sensed this and responded in kind!

Chapter Five

What's Your Dog Telling You?

It's the silence that makes me look up. Skye's presence in the room has been quiet but noticeable, punctuated by the occasional soft sigh, dream murmur, or shift of position, for the past hour, and I can't "feel" or hear him. I go to the back door, where he is patiently waiting to be let into the garden—as I knew he would be. Some dogs will bark to go out. Some scratch at the door or whine or nudge their owners. Skye is fully aware that he can communicate his needs and wishes without so much as a whimper.

Dogs have their own, very individual ways of letting us know what they want. They figure out the methods that work best through noticing what we respond to and what we ignore. If the desired result is forthcoming they will repeat the behavior. Skye knows that I can always tell when he wants to go outside, but if I ignored the sudden silence he would find another strategy—most likely a whimper or a woof—to get my attention. Your dog will have his own method, and noticing what this is will ensure that the floor stays puddle-free.

Dogs are experts at communicating, as you saw in chapter 3: "Body Language and Communication." When we observe them and take notice of what they're telling us, the bond deepens. The ability to communicate effectively with a creature from a different species is a real privilege. After all, some of us find it difficult to be fluent in another human language, so "speaking dog" and seeing the pleasure on our dogs' faces when we "get" what they're saying is very exciting. It can be easy to take this for granted through long-term associations with our dogs, yet what is happening is really quite extraordinary.

Observing your dog's body language and signals, listening to him, paying attention to what is going on in his mind benefits both of you. Communication is the foundation for all relationships, whether these are human or canine, and good communication makes it possible to overcome even the rocky patches that may crop up occasionally.

Sometimes the signals get muddled, rather like a radio wavelength that has slipped a little and turned to static. Misinterpretation or confusion blocks the signals. When this happens, when you're not reading or hearing each other clearly, it's time to slow down, to listen to your feelings instead of getting frustrated by striving to figure things out. Often, when you just relax and ask yourself what your dog is really trying to tell you, when you look at his body language or listen to his voice and gauge what the feeling is behind all of this, the answer becomes clear.

Your dog has been strongly influenced by his early environment. He has inherited certain characteristics through his breed or mix of breed. If he was bred from a line of working dogs and they have been used for that purpose, he will inherit that intensely focused working spirit. Two of the Cocker Spaniels I have known since they were puppies look very similar, and they're both active, cheerful dogs whose greatest pleasure when outside is to run around in ever-widening circles, tails wagging at top speed, sniffing everything in their path. One of these was bred as a show dog, and the other came from working parents. Both dogs were brought home to be pets, yet the offspring of working parents wore his owners to a frazzle while he was growing up, because his desire to fulfill his natural purpose was being hampered and he was using up his pent-up energy by literally running rings around them. His behavior was his way of telling his owners that he needed a job to do, and once they realized this and found acceptable outlets for his energy, he and they were happy.

The breed of dog and his inbred instincts define his behavior to a large degree, though every dog is an individual and it would be unwise to expect a certain type of personality simply because a dog is of a particular breed. The widespread opinion of Pit Bulls and Staffordshire Bull Terriers, for instance, is sadly mostly negative, yet many are devoted family pets. Whatever the breed, your dog is a dog and will display inherent instinctive doggy behavior. For instance, most dogs love to play with fluffy toys because this activity harks back to chasing and catching prey. Terriers will grasp their fluffy toys by the back of the neck, shake them, and throw them aside because this is how they kill the small animals, such as rats, that they were bred to dispose of. However, other breeds do this, too. For Skye and for Shep, my Collie-Husky crossbreed foster dog, this is a great game!

The Cocker Spaniels from different backgrounds are just one example of how the early environment and heritage shape the dog. This is why it's important to find out as much as you can about your dog's past, although, if that is unknown, you can often guess at some of this by his behavior and reactions. The combination of breed, inborn instincts and whether these were consciously developed by the people who were present during the first weeks, basic temperament, and previous and current environmental conditions all have a powerful effect on a dog's personality. When you combine these elements and look at how your dog acts and reacts, you can gain an in-depth insight into what drives him, motivates him, unnerves him, and makes him happy. This will make it much easier for you to work out what he's telling you when he deliberately engages you in communication.

THE GIFT OF LISTENING

We live in a busy, noisy world. In our society pressure is an accepted part of life. Deadlines, meetings, and social events involve an outpouring of energy. How often do you have the opportunity to stop, be silent, observe, and simply listen? Finding the time to do this is vital in our relationships with the dogs in our lives—and with the people, too!

Listening takes two forms: passive and active. Passive listening is simply "being there" and noticing what's going on without responding in any way other than giving your undivided attention to your dog. It involves allowing the behavior to take place; observing it; and noticing the signals, the body language, and/or the vocal tones without interfering or succumbing to the urge to do something about it. Active listening involves interaction—giving nonverbal cues, through your facial expressions and body language, that act as feedback and using your voice too, so that a conversation comes into being.

When you really listen, you pick up subtle cues that provide more information about what your dog is conveying to you. This is a gift for both of you because it enables the channels of communication between you to be more open. Conversation through the voice and the body transforms into dialogue, the building of a connection in which each of you learns from the other in an atmosphere of mutual respect. When clear communication becomes a two-way street, you can know immediately, without even having to think much about it, what your dog is conveying to you. It becomes instinctive and automatic.

TELLING SIGNALS

Your dog will have his own ways of letting you know that he needs to go outside or would love to play or go for a walk or is hungry. Dogs enjoy a certain amount of routine, and if you're late preparing a meal, he'll soon let you know! He may pace, sniff the floor, circle, whine, or bark when he needs to go out for a toilet break. He may drop a toy at your feet or dance around when he wants to play. Perhaps he fetches his leash or stands hopefully close by it to ask for a walk. And he's likely to wait by his bowl or in the food preparation area when dinnertime has slipped your mind.

It's easy to see when your dog is acting up. He may even develop his personal repertoire in order to convey his feelings or catch your attention. He may chew forbidden objects or grab and run off with them. He may nudge, scratch, whine, pester you or another companion animal, or find any number of ways in which to release energy or capture your attention. Some of this, especially with puppies, is due to a sense of mischief or an abundance of energy, or simply that he hasn't yet learned the house rules so everything is a game. In an adult dog, undesirable behavior can be due to boredom or frustration, so adding more interest and stimulation to his daily life can bring unwanted behaviors to a halt. A game in between walk times will reduce pent-up energy and provide some fun for both of you. A chew toy or a food-filled Kong will keep him occupied while you are out or busy and provide comfort through chewing. Kongs also enable much-needed mental stimulation because your dog has to figure out how to get to the food stuffed inside it.

Most owners instinctively know when their dog is unwell. He may lose interest in food, walks, or games; he may be unusually quiet; his tail may wag less than usual; or he may whine or yelp if he's in pain. As we get to know our dogs, we often notice a subtle difference in demeanor even before the tell-tale signs of illness are apparent. The invisible threads of affection and familiarity that link us can act as a telegraph line, allowing us to receive messages that aren't apparent to other people. If you feel at all concerned about your dog's health, even if there are no obvious signs of illness, listen to your feelings and ask your veterinary surgeon to check him over.

Dogs can give out similar signals to those of ill health when something is bothering them. Changes in circumstances or routine often cause dogs to seem unhappy, under the weather. or generally quiet and out of sorts while they try to understand and process these changes. They may lose their appetites or pace or whine. Understanding that your dog is reacting to something that causes him stress will make you feel more compassionate toward him, and investigating the possible causes will enable you to find a solution.

Combining the arts of observation and listening can help you to understand how and why your dog acts and reacts as he does. If you see that he is nervous or afraid, you can take steps to calmly reassure him or to move him away from the source of his emotional discomfort. This builds his confidence in you and helps him to work through stressful situations more easily.

New experiences are wholeheartedly welcomed by some dogs and are a cause of great anxiety for others. Your dog's responses are based on his personality type and his past experiences. An outgoing, confident dog will embrace opportunities for new stimuli, whereas an introverted dog, or one who has had negative experiences in the past, may be fearful of anything new. Your ability to read your dog, to listen to him on every level, is beneficial for both of you. It means that you understand him and can take appropriate action, and he sees that you are in tune with him so he feels safer in your presence. The bonds of mutual trust are further strengthened.

AN EXERCISE IN WATCHING

As part of their studies in canine psychology, I ask my students to go to a place such as a dog park, to observe the interactions that are taking place, and to make detailed notes for a subsequent essay. They can video this, too, if they wish, as playing back the video later on gives far more information on interactions that could otherwise be missed. You can try this as a fun exercise because it gives fascinating insights into the dynamics of different relationships. However, for this personal exercise you will be observing and assessing your own dog.

When you take your dog out, watch how he behaves. Is he eager for new sights and smells, or does he prefer to hang out around familiar spots where he can catch up on news? Observe how he responds to other dogs and how they in turn respond to him. Does he want to move forward and get to know other dogs, or does he hang back or stay close to your side? Is he more comfortable on or off his leash? Are his reactions the same toward every dog he meets, or does he change these according to the other dog?

Next, observe your dog's interactions with people. Dogs can sniff out a caring or hostile person very easily, and your dog's reactions can tell you a great deal about the other person as well as your dog. They know when someone is a "dog" person and tend to respond with clear signals of excitement or affection. Are there people who he particularly likes? If so, why do you think this is? Perhaps their affinity with dogs shines through, even if they're not making a fuss of your dog, or maybe they have a kind word or a treat for your dog, so a positive association is created.

If your dog seems uncomfortable around certain people, ask yourself why this is. Perhaps they don't like dogs or are afraid of them (as with John's case history in chapter 4: "How Your Dog Reads You"). Maybe they speak too loudly or move jerkily or give hard, thumping pats instead of gentle strokes, so this makes your dog anxious. They may be in a bad mood or are unpredictable. Or they may be giving out subtle signals of antipathy toward you that your dog is picking up on.

Alongside all of this, observe what makes your dog happy. Look, too, at whether this is the quiet kind of happiness that manifests as a softly wagging tail, bright eyes. and a doggy smile or that exuberant joyful happiness that your dog displays when he is play-bowing, dancing with glee, or wagging his tail like a flag in high winds. Ask yourself who seems to be his favorite person, and why this could be. See which food he likes best, and whether he goes through phases of preferring one food or toy over another.

Think about your findings, and you may be surprised at how easy it is to understand what your dog is telling you. This knowledge can be learned, but this ability to read others, both human and animal, is also contained within the instinctive element of your psyche that was part of the survival kit of your far distant ancestors. When you consciously look and listen, you are able to attune to the subtle, as well as obvious, signals, and you acquire a special kind of wisdom that is based on simple attunement. This will change your relationships with every dog you encounter in the future.

Your dog can tell you a great deal about yourself, too. His approach and his attitude toward you in any given moment is an indicator of the energy that you are "giving out." You have probably noticed that your dog avoids you or demonstrates conciliatory behaviors when you are feeling irritable or annoyed. When you feel good, he'll make it clear that he wants to be close to you or to play. When you feel sad, he may lie beside you and give sympathetic looks.

Dogs are like emotional sponges and are strongly affected by our states of mind because they are so aware of how we are feeling. Because of this, if there is no apparent reason why your dog is suddenly following you or avoiding you, perhaps the answer lies within you rather than him. If so, taking steps to change your mood will also lead to a change in his behavior.

Your relationship with your dog is greatly enhanced when you can listen to what he's telling you. Potentially difficult situations can be averted because you are able to see that your dog is becoming uncomfortable or ill at ease. More fun can be had because you know what makes his tail wag. And the bond between you grows increasingly stronger because you are both taking sure steps toward increased mutual understanding.

CASE HISTORY: SALLY

Sally, a six-year-old Golden Retriever, was an easygoing dog in every respect except one. Although bred from a line of gun dogs, she was terrified of loud noises and had been passed on to her current owners as a young adolescent because she couldn't be used as a working dog.

Sally's home was quiet. She lived with a gentle older couple whose children had grown up and left home. Sally greeted visitors with pleasure and had no objection to music or the television, but during thunderstorms or firework displays or when hunters could be heard shooting in the distance, she would cringe, whine, and fit herself as tightly under the bed as possible, often staying there for hours after hearing the noise that had disturbed her. In her terror she would often wet herself, and nothing would induce her to come out from her hiding place.

I decided to use two methods that could help Sally to cope, and we began her rehabilitation at a quiet time when she was under no stress. First I tempted Sally to move toward me from her bed, which was a place of safety for her, by looking away in order to show I was no threat. I placed a piece of chicken on the floor, just out of her reach, calling her name softly as I did so. As chicken was a rare treat, Sally soon moved forward to take it and then waited, tail wagging hopefully, in case more was forthcoming. Another piece of chicken was placed slightly further away, so that Sally came out to eat it—and received lots of praise. Sally's owners would use this only when Sally hid under their bed in the future.

The next step was to accustom Sally to the noises of which she was so afraid. We played recordings of these at a very low volume, barely audible, and each time Sally showed signs of stress or anxiety, we lowered the volume even more. This had to be done at a pace that was comfortable for Sally; otherwise it wouldn't work. As Sally learned to gradually tolerate the sounds at low volume, we praised and treated her, scratched behind her ears (which she loved), and then raised the level very slightly. Her owners observed her carefully to watch for the slightest signs of discomfort. Eventually Sally could wander around the room without showing any signs of stress when she heard the sounds at full volume.

One school of thought in dog behavior recommends that you ignore your dog when he is showing signs of stress, as reassurance would prompt the dog to repeat the behavior. This seems cruel to me—after all, would you ignore your beloved child if he was frightened? The Sympatico method recommends that you give gentle reassurance in the form of soft words and a light touch on the shoulder or back. Sally's owners used this whenever Sally showed the first signs of fear—lowered body posture, ears pinned back, and a low whine were Sally's initial signals of distress—and doing this helped to defuse her tension before it had chance to escalate into a full-blown terror reflex.

It took two weeks for Sally to completely ignore the sounds that had previously terrified her. During that time she hid beneath the bed only twice and could be coaxed out with soft words and pieces of chicken. After that, Sally no longer reacted to the noises that had caused her such distress in the past.

Chapter Six

Who's Training Whom?

I've been working at my desk for some time, while the dogs sleep close by my feet. Shep ("The Shepster"), my fifteen-year-old foster dog, opens his eyes and struggles to get up. Shep only recently came to live with us, and his atrophied leg muscles make walking almost impossible. Although his back legs often let him down, his mind is as clear as a bell and nothing gives him more pleasure than a cuddle. He soaks up love like a sponge and gives it back in abundance. The Shepster will live with us for his final weeks or months, as his health issues rule out rehoming.

After a brief battle with gravity and a couple of false starts, all four paws are planted reasonably firmly on the ground. The Shepster puts his head on one side, smiles wolfishly at me, and waits. I stop what I'm doing and go to sit on the floor beside him, one arm around his thick ruff while my free hand gently rubs behind his ears. He nuzzles against me, licks my arm, and makes the purring sound that means all is good in his world. Shep has trained me well, and I'm a willing accomplice. This dear old boy deserves the best that I can offer him throughout his twilight time.

The deep affection that has developed between The Shepster and me in just a short time has helped to make training reciprocal. He knows that hugs are there for the asking, and his trust makes him cooperative when I help him work through his issues. You can find out about Shep's extraordinary progress in his success story in part III.

With The Shepster, I used the affection he craved in order to build his trust, and his subsequent confidence in me made it possible for him to overcome his worst fear—the big outdoors. Some "person training" is unacceptable—I won't allow dogs to beg for my food, for instance, as being pestered while eating is a real nuisance. You'll find out how to stop this later in this chapter, in the section on "sneaky training."

There's a tendency to think that it's always the humans who train their dogs, and certainly we spend a great deal of time teaching our dogs to behave in ways that we find desirable or acceptable. However, training is a two-way street. We need the cooperation of our dogs for training to be effective and long-lasting, and the best way to ensure cooperation is to gain the dog's trust and affection and to make training fun so that he'll want to pay attention. Yet dogs train us, too! Shep knows that I'll respond to a certain look, and I do—because it feels good to make this sweet elderly dog happy in such a simple way.

If you stop what you're doing and walk your dog because he's pacing and whining or dropping the lead at your feet, you've been well-trained by your four-legged friend. If you serve dinner early because you've noticed him looking eagerly at his bowl; if you give him scraps from the table at meal-times; if you cut short a phone call because your dog is acting up; or if you decide to cancel a date because he may be lonely at home—well then, your training is progressing very nicely from his point of view!

When Skye was a puppy, he devised some very effective ways to get my attention when I was on the phone. Mostly he would bark or whine, making it hard to hear the other person. Nibbling the edge of the table also worked quite well, and years later, my coffee table still bore the souvenir imprints of tiny sharp teeth. One time he bit through the telephone cord in one speedy pounce while I was talking—literally cutting off the conversation. As I wasn't open to being trained in this way, he soon learned that the silent "stop" signal, hand up and palm outward, meant that no more distraction methods were allowed, and he would then lie down quietly. One of the complaints I hear frequently from owners is that their dogs act up as soon as the phone rings. I can hear the dog barking in the background while the owner tries to shout above the noise, and that brings back memories of short-lived puppy antics. It must be strange to a dog that we pick up a piece of plastic and talk to ourselves when it calls to us, and it must be immensely satisfying for him to be able to distract us!

DON'T SWEAT THE SMALL STUFF

The "alpha wolf" training that is based on dominance and hierarchy makes it clear that you should never, ever pander to the wishes of your dog. The theory goes that if you do this the dog gains the upper hand (or paw) and becomes the boss. The Sympatico method recommends consistency in train-ing, but gives more leeway regarding the "small stuff" that doesn't really inconvenience you. It allows you to set your own terms for the give-and-take that is a natural component in any successful relationship. To constantly be at the beck and call of our dogs would be counterproductive for them and for us and could render ineffective the important training that is necessary to having a well-behaved dog. But our relationship with dogs is based on effective communication, and sometimes it does no harm to give attention when it is asked for, as long as we don't teach our dogs to be pushy and annoying.

The most important issue, however, is that this must be our choice—so that we don't feel coerced into stopping whatever we are doing because our dog is being demanding. Simply put, if you want to give attention, give it— and if you don't want to (or are busy), then use a signal that shows your dog that this is not the right time for you.

Your signal could be to say, "Not now," or to hold out your hand in a "stop" position or to shake your head and carry on with your current task or to point to your dog's bed so that he knows to go there. Your dog will soon learn that this signal means that playtime, walk time, or snuggle time is postponed until it's convenient for you.

Your dog observes you closely and constantly, even when you're not aware of this. Walk past your seemingly asleep dog, and his eyes will open immediately. Show him you're free to play, through minute changes in your facial expression or body language, and he will gleefully solicit a game. Likewise, he knows when you're not willing or able to interact with him, if you teach him specific signals. Through being consistent in your use of these signals at inopportune times, he will soon immediately "get" what you are saying to him and will automatically follow through on this.

YOUR DOG'S SNEAKY TRAINING

Often our dogs train us in insidious ways. I call this "sneaky training" be- cause we may not even notice that we're being manipulated. If you have taught your dog to do something, such as give a paw in exchange for praise or a treat, you may find that he falls back on this when he's confused about what you want from him. Perhaps you're aiming to teach him to sit up on his butt and offer both paws. You give the signal for this, but your dog doesn't understand. Instead, he goes through the repertoire of what he has already learned. He may give a paw and look hopefully at you, but this isn't what you want. So you wait. He gives the other paw. He stands up or lies down. You use the new signal again. Eventually your dog rises high enough that both front paws are off the ground—and he gets the praise and treat.

So far, so good—he has learned what you wanted. However, if he's feeling that a treat would be nice right now, he's likely to perform the action that is usually rewarded with a treat—except that, this time, you didn't ask it of him. He may trot over to you, sit, and offer a paw. That "Awww" feeling you have when he does this may prompt you to give him what he's asking for. If so, you have been sneakily trained!

One day I stopped in the street to chat with a friend who has a beautiful Greyhound called Paddy. He's a calm, well-behaved boy, and he stood quietly beside us for a few minutes after I had greeted him. Then he raised a front paw and poked at his owner. Without pausing in what she was saying or looking at him, she put her hand in her pocket and took out a treat. Paddy snaffled it. A moment later the paw nudged her again, and another treat was given. After the third time, I was laughing out loud. "You have a very clever dog," I told her. She looked surprised, until I explained how well Paddy was using sneaky training on her. Personally I would have stopped responding to Paddy's demands and ended the behavior—she must get through a lot of treats in one day through letting Paddy demand them, and ultimately this wouldn't be good for his health. Also, she was taking on the role of servant, which isn't the relationship she wanted with her dog. But from then on, knowing what he was doing, Paddy's owner could make her own choice as to whether or not to let Paddy manipulate her.

Begging to share your food is very sneaky training. Those soft liquid eyes looking appealingly at you, perhaps an off-putting line of drool sliding toward your lap, butt-shuffles, plaintive whines, and sometimes full-on barking and determined lunging are all designed to convince you that your dog is starving hungry, even if he's just had a meal. Dogs are opportunist eaters—if there's an opportunity, they will eat! If you succumb, even once, to the temptation to offer a morsel, you will set yourself up to be pestered every time you want to eat anything.

Every rescue dog who has come to stay with me has begged mercilessly for food at first. Some of the dogs have been starved and are horribly emaciated, so they get small, frequent meals to build up their strength and gradually increase their weight. Even so, my meals are never shared with them. The large dogs who can reach the kitchen counter often try the "clean sweep" method, using paws and tongues to clear the area swiftly. Some dogs are a reasonable weight or are overweight because they have been fed table snacks between meals, but they still try out sneaky training during the first day.

The solution to this is very simple. Don't ever feed a dog from your plate, however persistent he is, and don't allow the dog to help himself from the kitchen counter. If your dog tries to jump up, turn away, step sideways to block his access, and carry on with preparing the meal. You may have to do this repeatedly for a day or two, but dogs swiftly learn that there's no point in trying to mug you for extra food. Of course, if you leave food lying around, within reach and unattended, it's considered fair game to your dog! If your dog begs while you're eating, direct him to his bed or an area of the floor away from you. Initially you can do this by throwing a treat (not from your plate) to the area you want him to go to and saying, "On your bed" or "Lie down" as soon as he goes to that area. Before long he'll stop bothering you at mealtimes.

It can help to start teaching this to your dog when you're eating something that doesn't smell too tempting for him. You could try it when you have some toast or cereal. From there, you can graduate to training him while you eat foods that he really would love to share with you. A dog with polite manners at human mealtimes is much nicer to be around.

TWO-WAY TRAINING

We train our dogs. They train us, if we allow them to. And during these processes both sides are learning about the other. By observing your responses to what your dog is doing, you'll discover how far his training of you is progressing. If you're feeling irritated or manipulated, it's time to change your response by ignoring the behavior, turning away, or sending him temporarily to his bed. If the two-way training is working well for you, it's fine to let it carry on.

Asking yourself what is rewarding to your dog, and why, can help you to understand your dog's little quirks. This makes it much easier to reduce and then eliminate unwanted behaviors. If you are responding with your voice, a look, a treat, or even by speaking sharply, your dog is gaining your attention. Bearing this in mind helps you to decide whether it's acceptable for the behavior to continue, if it's not a problem for you, or whether it's time to step in and refuse to be trained.

DOG TO DOG TRAINING

Dogs can train other dogs, too. Annie, one of my friends, has four dogs. Maisy, a Jack Russell Terrier who is almost thirteen, has figured out how to get Lucy, an eight-year-old Greyhound, to do her bidding at night. What makes this even more interesting is that although Maisy and Lucy get on well, they don't seem to be especially close. Of the two, Maisy is the stronger character and Lucy is rather quiet.

The dogs sleep in the bedroom with their owners. When Maisy needs a nighttime toilet break, she could easily wake her owners by barking or whining, as she does this during the day. Instead, she silently goes downstairs and waits by the back door. Lucy then barks to rouse Annie and goes straight back to bed as soon as Annie gets up to let Maisy out. Lucy never goes outside at night. Somehow Maisy has figured out a way to communicate to Lucy that she needs to go outside, and Lucy cooperates by waking her owners.

Research has shown that domestic dogs bond more strongly with humans than with other dogs, but dogs can also learn a great deal from the other dogs in their environment. Puppies learn how to be dogs through observing, and interacting with, their parents and elders. Anxious dogs can benefit from the company of a calm dog, as this gives them more confidence. If you teach your dog a new trick in the presence of another dog, it's likely that the second dog will pick it up, too. If one dog barks when the doorbell rings, any other dogs in the home are likely to join in. I use this co-learning principle with the traumatized foster dogs who come to stay with us. They can see that Skye is comfortable with me and that I treat him well. This, combined with gentle handling, helps them to settle in quickly.

WHO'S TRAINING WHOM?

By now you have most likely figured out the areas in which you train your dog and those in which your dog trains you. It can be amusing to see how eminently trainable we humans are and how effectively dogs can persuade us to do what they want us to do. Dogs can be excellent manipulators. Looking at the relationship, and understanding the subtle undertones that take place within this, can give us a (sometimes healthy and sometimes grudging) respect for the ability of dogs to use their considerable powers of persuasion on us!

CASE HISTORY: TILLY

When Tilly, one of my foster dogs, came to live with us, her behavior spoke volumes about the effects of her difficult past. Tilly, a dear little eleven-year-old Jack Russell Terrier, had been repeatedly abandoned and had been in and out of the dog pound countless times over a five-year period. It was love at first sight for both of us when she arrived, and she also quickly developed a strong attachment to my daughter, Amber, and to Skye. Dogs very quickly form powerful bonds with people who are kind to them, and Tilly was a classic example of a small dog with a huge heart.

Not surprisingly, little Tilly had separation anxiety. At first she was careful to never be more than a few inches from my side. She curled up in her bed beside my feet while I worked at the computer and snuggled up on my lap when I relaxed on the sofa in the evenings. After a while she expanded her horizons and would go in search of Amber, napping in her room while Amber studied.

Tilly had a real talent for making her feelings known. Her way of telling me that she was terrified of being abandoned yet again was to follow me constantly, ensuring that I was always in her line of vision. Although she developed a bond with Amber, at first she chose me as her rock, her secure base, in what had been a very confusing life for her.

Initially if I had to go out and leave her with Amber, Tilly cried pitifully and paced in the hallway, greeting me ecstatically as soon as I came home. I worked with this by going into another room, closing the door for a few seconds, and then returning, so that she would learn that she wasn't in danger of being abandoned just because she was alone for a moment.

If she felt that I had been working at the computer for too long and needed a break and a cuddle with her, she would stand beside me, look up, and "talk" in a funny squeaky voice that sounded just like a kazoo. I made a video of her doing this because it sounded so funny and her determination to get my attention was so clear. It worked for Tilly some of the time because the sight of her tiny face peering up at me and the sound of her croaky little voice made me helpless with laughter. However, it wasn't always convenient for me to stop what I was doing, so the solution was to talk back to her for a moment, acknowledging her and allowing the conversation to flow between us, and then nod in the direction of her bed and carry on working. Tilly soon got the message.

Tilly was devoted to Skye and followed him everywhere, making her kazoo noise to persuade him to give her attention. Skye, who was easily two feet taller than Tilly, discovered that the only place that Tilly couldn't reach was up on my daughter's bed, and so he would go there for a break when Tilly's adoration got too exhausting. Once he was on the bed, Tilly understood that any interaction was over for a while and wandered off to find something else to do.

For Tilly, the reward for vocalizing was attention, and she used it to her utmost. Yet she learned that there were times when the desired attention wasn't forthcoming, and she soon understood the signals that meant it was time to entertain herself.

Sadly, Tilly's kidneys failed and she passed away while she was with us. The memory of this endearing little dog with such a huge character always makes me smile when I think of her.

II

When Two Hearts Beat as One

Chapter Seven

The Sympatico Method versus Dominance Methods

Skye and I are out walking. He's eighteen months old, and we're living in the city of Bath at this time. A woman walks toward us with her full-grown male Akita. Skye, keen to make friends, does a little leap into the air and pulls on his leash. I stop, so he stops and his leash goes loose. Skye waits for me to move forward, and I stay still, seeing that the other dog's body language isn't friendly. The Akita is on an extending leash and he's way ahead of his owner, dragging her toward us as he snarls and shows his teeth. The woman has lost all semblance of control and is being helplessly pulled along by her dog.

Fortunately the road is clear, so I quickly tell Skye, "Let's go," and cross to the other side of the road. As I walk away, Skye close beside me, I hear the woman yelling at her dog to try to get him under control. I look back just as she slaps him on the rump. The Akita is learning that the presence of other dogs means pain, and he's likely to be even more antagonistic toward fellow canines in the future.

Dogs learn how to respond to people and other dogs through the training and cues they received (or didn't receive) from their owners. There has been a great deal of controversy over how dogs should be trained, and during recent years a major divide has emerged in the area of dog training. On one side of the fence are trainers and behaviorists who believe that dogs are constantly trying to dominate us, doing whatever they can to set the rules in our relationships with them. The reasoning behind, and effectiveness of "dominance theory," as this is called, has been scientifically disproved, yet the myths behind it are still being perpetuated in some quarters, and it has become something of a celebrity cult. Cesar Millan, the charismatic "Dog Whisperer," is one of the best-known proponents of the dominance methods.

On the other side of the fence is what I call the Sympatico method. The principles in this are in accordance with what is known as "positive training" and "compassionate training." This is now endorsed by scientists specializing in research into dogs' minds and behavior. They dispute the old dominance theory with firm evidence that dogs are *not* trying to gain control over humans; they are simply trying to cope in a world that is very different from the one in which they evolved. The Sympatico method, in essence, means "to be in sympathy and harmony" with the dog. It works through teaching the dog to trust his owner and to choose to cooperate rather than have to be forced or coerced. Victoria Stilwell, the dog trainer whose series *It's Me or the Dog* is on Animal Planet, is one of the best-known proponents of positive dog training. Another is Zak George, whose shows on Animal Planet and the BBC reveal how easy and fun it can be to train dogs with positive methods.

Clearly these two methods are directly opposed to each other, and both methods have a powerful effect on the relationship between dog and owner. So what are the main differences between them, and how do they affect our dogs? Here are some examples of Dominant Leadership and the Sympatico method. Which would you prefer to have used on you?

DOMINANT LEADERSHIP ON "ALPHA DOGS"

According to this theory, dogs behave like wolves and are constantly striving to increase their ranking in their "pack" through the use of intimidation and aggression. Therefore, we humans must become the "alpha dog" (forceful leader of the pack) and continually assert a ranking system that places the human at the top. This is often seen literally as the human standing over the dog because it's considered that a dog will show dominance by standing over another dog or by placing his head over another dog's neck.

According to this method, as the "alpha" animal the human eats first, goes through doorways first, and uses force and punishment in order to gain obedience. Any misdemeanors or lapses are dealt with immediately through (often harsh) correction, in order to teach the dog that the human is the "alpha" and will not tolerate any misbehavior. The theory behind Dominant Leadership is that dogs are constantly searching for ways in which they can dominate the humans around them and will take advantage of any opportunity to do so. For instance, a dog who jumps up is viewed as attempting to be "higher" than the human, as an assertion of rank. In fact, most often the dog is merely giving an overexuberant greeting, much as puppies will greet the mother by licking her face to solicit food or to indicate submissiveness. Some particularly "pushy" dogs are like unruly teenagers who haven't been taught good manners, so will demand attention by jumping up and even by grabbing clothing or an arm. This isn't dominance, but it's a mark of a dog who hasn't been taught acceptable ways of behaving. A dog who pulls on the lead is assumed to be trying to lead the "pack" and be the "alpha," rather than simply being excited about the new sights, smells, and sounds around him.

THE SYMPATICO METHOD ON "ALPHA DOGS"

Unfortunately, the proponents of the "wolf theory" have ignored the fact that the dominance theory is based on studies of *captive/managed* wolf packs, which behave very differently from wild wolf packs. There is far more aggression between captive wolves because they have been forced into an unnatural situation, having to live in proximity to other wolves who are not family members. In the wild there is enmity between different wolf packs because they are in direct competition with each other for resources that enhance their chances of survival. To try to make comparisons between wild wolves, captive wolves, and domestic dogs is not only misguided—it's ludicrous. Science has proven that dogs are not wolves in different coats; the dog has evolved alongside humans, and their brains work very differently from those of wolves. As Dr. John Bradshaw, founder of the Anthrozoology Institute and a founder of the International Society for Anthrozoology (ISAZ), said in *Woof! A Horizon Guide to Dogs*, a television program about our relationships with dogs, "We have changed the way their brains work."

In fact, our dogs are not interested in ruling us. They want to live harmoniously with us, as we are the providers of their shelter, food, and social interaction—all of which are essential to their well-being. Our role, therefore, should be that of guide and guardian. We give guidance, companionship, and affection, and we ensure their needs are met. And we need to set the important house rules; otherwise our lives would be chaos. Our world is a confusing place to dogs, and like children, they are our responsibility and need boundaries and guidelines.

With the Sympatico method, we choose reward-based methods that teach the dog to trust us and to willingly cooperate, instead of using force, which would create a relationship based on fear. Any method that creates fear or stress for the dog is to be avoided because no creature is able to learn while in a state of high stress—the response to fear and stress is to either become overreactive or to shut down altogether. The training we do with our dogs is best absorbed and remembered when the dog is in a positive receptive state.

If a dog jumps up, the owner can stop this by turning away. As jumping is a plea for attention and a greeting, the greeting is not given until the dog is calm, with all four paws on the ground. If a dog is pulling on the lead, the owner either turns in the opposite direction so the dog has to follow or gets the dog's focus with food or toy rewards so that the dog follows the hand carrying the tantalizing resource. Praise and rewards are given each time the dog walks nicely. Often the dog can be trained without the need for commands. If you want your dog to calm down at feeding time, you can simply wait until he's calm and then serve the meal, instead of telling him to sit. Dogs soon learn what's expected of them, especially when their actions lead to a reward.

DOMINANT LEADERSHIP ON EXERCISE

Dominance proponents say that dogs need to have their energy "drained" by exercising them to exhaustion. They need a brisk run, walk/jog, or bike ride as a way of starting the day, with no stops for sniffing, so they will obey their owners or desist from destructive tendencies when left alone. This is followed by another bout of brisk exercise later on. The use of a treadmill at speed is also considered to be good for the dog.

All dogs need exercise in order to be healthy and to maintain their weight and muscle tone. However, too much exercise can be as detrimental as too little. This method doesn't take into consideration the fact that dogs need time to stop and sniff around, to stroll rather than be forced to trot, as they gain a great deal of information and mental stimulation through using their senses and in particular identifying and absorbing scents. Overexercising young dogs can affect their physical health, too, and is a major cause of muscle strains, bone problems, and early onset arthritis.

THE SYMPATICO METHOD ON EXERCISE

Dogs need a certain amount of exercise to maintain fitness, and two or three walks each day of a length of time that's appropriate for the breed, age, and fitness of the dog works best for them. If this isn't possible, one good walk will keep your dog in shape and give him all-important sensory stimulation. Greyhounds, for instance, generally need only twenty to thirty minutes of walking twice daily, whereas a Collie or Jack Russell Terrier may need two to three hours of exercise daily, as well as playtime with a ball or Frisbee. As a general rule, the working breeds (Collies, Spaniels, German Shepherds, Terriers) need more exercise than the sprinters (Sighthounds) or lapdogs. Even with these dogs, a Collie would have periods of rounding up sheep and periods of rest. Ratting terriers, such as Jack Russells, use bursts of energy.

In the wild a dog would gain this exercise by searching for food and would not choose to travel miles each day unless it were necessary. If you "drain" a dog's energy, you simply have an exhausted and overstimulated dog who cannot unwind and relax afterward. Interestingly, one of the remedies for a hyperactive dog in the Sympatico method is to *reduce* the amount of exercise in order to teach the dog to relax. A dog who is getting the right amount of exercise for his breed, age, and energy level is much happier and healthier than an overexercised dog.

DOMINANT LEADERSHIP ON SOCIALIZING WITH OTHER DOGS

Dogs are social creatures, and they have their own version of doggy manners. This involves using body language to approach each other in such a way as to show other dogs that they are not a threat. Dog-aggressive dogs have most likely experienced fear in the past, often through being subjected to an attack from another dog, or they may have been inadequately socialized as puppies, so didn't have the opportunity to learn the signals that tell other dogs that they are friendly. This is not taken into account in dominance theory.

In the Dominant Leadership method, dogs that are aggressive or fearful with other dogs are thrust into a group of dogs so that the other dogs can "teach them to behave." This actually puts pressure on and intimidates the dog who is most likely aggressive because he is afraid. This is a recipe for creating extreme fear and further aggression in the long term. Dogs do learn from each other, but need an environment in which they can feel safe before they can learn to respond positively to other dogs. If you imagine being thrust into a group of people who make you feel scared or nervous, and they all crowd around you to find out who you are, this will give you an idea of how stressful this method is for dogs who are already reactive, anxious, or highly strung.

THE SYMPATICO METHOD ON SOCIALIZING WITH OTHER DOGS

Introducing a reactive dog to other dogs should be done calmly and gradually, and initially at a distance. This teaches the dog that no harm will come to him. The process involves turning in the opposite direction and moving away from the other dog if the sensitive dog reacts. The owner ignores the presence of the other dog, so that the reactive dog doesn't pick up that there's a problem—often owners will tense up at the sight of another dog, thereby making their own dog tense, too. Every sign of calm behavior is rewarded, and the dog is not moved closer to the other dog until his body language reveals that he does not feel stressed. Close observation of body language is used by the people, so that any signs of stress can be instantly seen and acted upon.

Initially both dogs are walked on leads at a distance with which the reactive dog is comfortable. The people walk on the inside, so that their bodies act as shields or barriers between the dogs. The Sympatico leader gradually lessens the distance between both dogs only after the dog is no longer reacting and his body language is relaxed. When the reactive dog looks comfortable, even during closer proximity, the people move position so that the dogs are on the inside, walking parallel to each other. When both dogs display signals that they wish to greet each other, they are allowed to do so, with the owners moving the dogs closer in a curving motion or with the reactive dog being moved behind the other dog for some polite butt-sniffing. This enables the dog to take the polite route for greeting another dog, helps him to feel safe and secure with his owner, and allows him to overcome his fears at a pace that is comfortable for him.

DOMINANT LEADERSHIP ON PUNISHMENT

According to Dominant Leadership principles, dogs are to be severely punished for their misdemeanors. For instance, the trainer or owner will do the "alpha roll" on the dog, whereby he is flipped onto his back and forcibly pinned down by the throat, to make the dog submit if he displays any signs of aggression. YouTube videos show Cesar Millan using methods such as deliberately provoking a frightened dog by poking him, in order to get an aggressive reaction so that he can harshly "correct" the aggression.

Punishment creates fear and resentment. Violence sets the scene for violent reactions. Dogs often don't understand what they have done wrong—because in their view, they aren't doing anything wrong. They have short memories for associations between their actions and our responses, so any correction needs to be carried out *while the behavior is taking place*, rather than ten minutes or an hour afterward. If dogs are punished harshly, they will view humans as unpredictable creatures who inflict pain on them for no apparent reason. Is this the relationship that you would want with your dog?

THE SYMPATICO METHOD ON PUNISHMENT

The Sympatico method avoids punishment. This doesn't mean that dogs are allowed to misbehave without correction—rules and boundaries are important so that the environment is harmonious, but these should be made clear to the dog. If there is a serious infringement, such as a dog acting out of control, discipline in the form of a brief "time-out" for no more than two minutes may be employed. Discipline is only used when absolutely necessary. Distraction or diversion techniques, followed by rewards as soon as there is a shift to more appropriate behavior, work well for most misdemeanors.

Dogs will only repeat behaviors that they find rewarding. Reinforcement drives behavior. If the rewards stop, the dog sees no point in carrying on with that behavior. We tend to inadvertently reward dogs by, for instance, giving a dog attention when he is being demanding, by telling him to stop or be quiet. If we turn away or walk away, the reward of our attention is removed and the behavior eases and then ceases altogether.

In my work, some of the dogs with the reported worst aggression issues are those whose owners have used the "alpha roll" on them for growling or overexuberant behavior. This is actually detrimental for both dog and owner, and you will find out about the effects in the case histories at the end of this chapter. After all, a growl is a warning, and if you take forceful steps to remove that warning signal, the dog with no escape route feels he has no choice but to make his fear or irritation clear by biting the person who is not listening to his request for space.

DOMINANT LEADERSHIP ON WALKING ETIQUETTE

Proponents of dominance methods respond to a dog pulling on the lead by yanking the leash to lift the dog above the ground ("hanging"), supposedly "teaching" the dog to walk to heel. Other methods that are used involve poking the dog or rudely nudging his rear end with a foot, a frequently seen move on *The Dog Whisperer* and that I often see people doing when I'm out with my dogs. Choke collars to cut off the oxygen supply and electric collars to shock the dog are also commonly used to achieve submission.

A while ago I went to observe an outdoor puppy class that was being held near the small village where I live. Twelve puppies of various breeds, aged between twelve weeks and nine months, were lined up with their owners in an enclosure created in a field. The trainer was a firm subscriber to Dominant Leadership. Each owner was asked to stand at the end of the line and call his or her puppy, to teach them to come. The trainer put each puppy on a long training lead and walked the pup toward the owner. Understandably, the puppies wanted to get to the owner as fast as possible because they had bonded with that person. Yet each time they tried to dash ahead, the trainer lifted the lead so that the puppies were raised by the throat, with only their back legs on the ground. To attempt to teach the "come" signal with "walking to heel" was both cruel and confusing to the puppies, but the trainer was determined to enforce his control over dogs who were sadly being set up to distrust humans.

THE SYMPATICO METHOD ON WALKING ETIQUETTE

Advocates of the Sympatico method understand that causing a dog pain and fear only make him want to get as far away from the pain-bringer as possible. It also destroys all trust between dog and owner. If a dog is pulling on the lead, it's because he hasn't been taught properly, and the only effective long-term method is to train the dog to *want* to be close to you.

If you keep your dog on a tight lead, this creates pressure, and the dog's natural instinct is to move away from that pressure and pull harder against the lead. This sets up a habit of pulling. There are several compassionate methods that can be used. One is to stand still as soon as the dog starts to pull. The dog will soon learn that pulling on the lead means he's not getting to where he wants to go and he will stop and wait for direction.

Another method is to turn in the opposite direction without tugging the lead so that, again, the dog realizes that the best way to get on with the walk is to stay close to you and not pull. The dog should be rewarded every time he gets it right, however brief this time may be. This creates a positive association for the dog—walking on a loose lead, instead of pulling, means that good things happen!

Yet another method (and the one I tend to use for serious pullers) is to have treats in your hand so that the dog is focused on you (the source of rewards) instead of on trying to pull ahead. Every time the dog stops pulling, he receives praise and a reward. It's also important to give your dog the opportunity for a good sniff around. This provides stimulation that's just as important as the physical exercise he receives during his walks.

DOMINANT LEADERSHIP ON HANDLING FEARFUL DOGS

Dominant leaders expose a fearful dog to "flooding," which forces the dog to endure large amounts of the stimulus that makes him frightened, in order to get him to react to a point where he "shuts down" and becomes too numb inside to continue reacting.

A dog afraid of loud noises, for instance, would be exposed to those noises at full volume until he stops responding. This is extraordinarily traumatic for a dog. Think of something you're terrified of, and imagine being forced to be confronted by this harsh method, with no means of escape. For instance, if you're phobic about spiders or snakes, imagine you're about to be thrown into a tank full of them and this will give you a perspective on your dog's feelings!

THE SYMPATICO METHOD ON HANDLING FEARFUL DOGS

A fearful dog needs to be taught that he can still feel safe, even when the source of that fear is present. This is done by exposing him to a very low level of the stimulus that is causing the fear and by rewarding him with praise and treats, or a game, while the stimulus is present. The level of exposure is then very gradually increased, at a pace that is comfortable for the dog.

For instance, for a fear of loud noises such as fireworks, a recorded version of that noise is played very softly and the dog is rewarded for not reacting. The volume is gradually increased, and at any signs of stress is reduced again, until the dog no longer reacts when the volume is turned up to loud. Playing that recording while the real-life noise is occurring can cover up the obvious differences. Clearly, this is conditioning at its most humane and, as it turns out, most effective!

THE IMPORTANCE OF RESPECT

We expect our dogs to respect us, to listen to us, and to follow through on what we require of them. A well-adjusted, well-behaved dog is a credit to his owner. He's friendly and well socialized with people and other dogs, and he pays attention to us when we ask him to. In short, he's a pleasure to be with.

Our relationship with our dogs is a two-way street. In order to gain their respect, it's important that we also respect them. This doesn't mean giving way to them—it means understanding the differences in how they think and behave and allowing them to be dogs, instead of humanizing them. The Sympatico method takes into account dogs' innate dogginess and looks for ways in which we can allow dogs to express their natures (after all, that's one of the reasons why we love them so!) while also teaching them good manners.

A DEEPER UNDERSTANDING

The Sympatico method is based on an in-depth understanding of the mind, instincts, and needs of the dog. These "positive" methods work. It may sometimes take a little more time to see the results, but the effects are long-term and very worthwhile. The Sympatico method fosters a harmonious relationship and mutual respect between owner and dog.

Quick fixes are rarely effective. If you had a deep wound, you would need sutures rather than sticking plaster—the plaster may hold the wound in place for a short while, but it would soon reopen and become infected. Only sutures would enable the wound to fully heal. Our approach to our dogs needs to be viewed as a lifelong commitment to doing all that we can to make life good for them and for us. After all, when we bring a dog into our homes, we do this with the awareness that we will be caring for him for many years to come. Being patient while we teach our dogs how to behave well ultimately brings rewards that carry on for a lifetime.

Through understanding why our dogs behave as they do—and through allowing ourselves to have a sense of wonder that a creature of another species has chosen to share his life with us in an interspecies relationship that has spanned thousands of years—we can appreciate and fully enjoy that bond.

The Sympatico method is really quite simple. It hinges on understanding and common sense. When clients are astonished that the solution to their dog's problem is so simple and effective (for instance, turning your back when your dog jumps up), I always laugh and tell them that this isn't rocket science. And it's fun to use these positive methods and to feel the bond between our dogs and ourselves grow stronger.

CASE HISTORIES: GYPSY AND BLACKWELL

Gypsy

Gypsy is a beautiful Lurcher, part Greyhound and part Doberman. He came into rescue as an adolescent because he was highly aggressive toward both people and dogs. Discussions with his previous owners revealed that Gypsy had been an exuberant puppy who was constantly leaping on his owners and who would growl if he was told off. His owners had dealt with this by using the "alpha roll" method on him for every misdemeanor, however minor. This involved throwing him onto his back and pinning him down by the throat. Unsurprisingly, Gypsy had soon learned that anyone approaching him most likely intended to hurt and frighten him and to possibly even threaten his life.

Progress with Gypsy through the Sympatico method was achieved one small step at a time because his fear-based aggression was severe, but he gradually learned that people and other dogs could be a source of pleasure and joy as well as of pain. He was fortunate to be adopted by a very patient couple who were willing to work with him long term, and he gradually learned that human hands brought kindness, rewards, and gentle touch. The damage to his psyche was so great that it took time for him to relax and enjoy the company of his new owners and their other dogs, but their patience ultimately paid off and he became devoted to them.

Blackwell

Blackwell is a gorgeous German Shepherd who had been abandoned. He was placed with a new owner in what seemed an ideal situation. However, when conflict broke out between Blackwell and another dog in the home, the owner grabbed Blackwell by the scruff of his neck and lifted him, yanking him away from the other dog. Blackwell turned on the source of his pain and growled a warning. It's a credit to his self-restraint that he resisted biting. The next day he was returned to the kennel, where he displayed marked signs of aggression toward many of the people who tried to approach him.

Blackwell waited a long time for his new home, while he was gently taught that no one in the environment meant to harm him. Only a few people whom he trusted were allowed to approach him at first, and he slowly learned that a hand near his head meant a food reward and a gentle stroke instead of violence. Eventually he was adopted by a new owner, who first spent a great deal of time with him, taking him for walks and treating him with great kindness before taking him to his forever home. He's now happily settled, with no issues.

Chapter Eight

Bringing Home Your New Dog: Getting It Right from the Start

Skye is eight weeks old when he comes to live with us. During the journey home he snuggles calmly in my daughter's lap, eyes bright with curiosity, squirming around occasionally to clamber up and lick Amber's face. He seems excited about the new life ahead of him, and we're thrilled that this cuddlesome bundle of black and white fur will be with us for the rest of his life.

Rearing an energetic, mischievous puppy is fun, as it should be. Training goes smoothly, with just a few rebellious hiccoughs when Skye reaches adolescence—and these, swiftly overcome, provide a great deal of amusement and contribute to the countless happy memories as Skye grows to maturity. We look back at his puppy photos sometimes, and our hearts melt all over again. Then we look at him now, five years old and all grown up, carrying himself with a dignity that sometimes gets sidelined by madcap antics and entertaining acts of sheer foolishness. Skye has been generous about sharing his family and home with many other dogs, some fostered, some adopted, and in many ways I consider him to be my muse.

It's easy to get it right from the start with a new dog when you know how. And this will open up a future enriched by years of companionship, countless belly laughs, hugs, fun and games, comforting licks when you feel down, and a dog's lifetime of love and unstinting devotion.

Whether you are buying a puppy from a reputable breeder or adopting a rescue dog from a shelter, the first few days of your new life together are crucial. They set the scene and lay down the groundwork for your future relationship. During this time you will be introducing your dog to new people and experiences, familiarizing him with his new environment, and setting the ground rules that will form the basis for his future training. You will be teaching your dog to trust you and pay attention to you and giving him plenty of opportunities to bond with you. If you use calm consistency, clear guidance and direction, and plenty of praise and rewards for desired behaviors, your new dog should quickly settle in and make himself at home.

It usually takes a few days for a dog to adjust to the shock of change and around two weeks for him to properly settle into his new home, to figure out what type of person you are, and to assess the "lay of the land" and figure out coping strategies at what is a stressful time for him.

When you bring a new dog into your home, you are effectively making a contract, a promise, to take care of him to the best of your ability. Some breeders and most rescue shelters insist you sign an actual contract that declares this intention, and there may also be a clause that states that the dog must be returned to the breeder or rescue if things don't work out. Even if there is no need to sign a piece of paper, you should be aware that your dog will be dependent on you to have all his needs met, and he will bond strongly with you in a very short space of time. A dog is a long-term commitment.

A PUPPY OR AN OLDER DOG?

Your age and lifestyle are prime considerations when you're deciding which dog would be most compatible. Puppies are hugely entertaining company, and it's a joy to watch them grow up and learn all about the world. Everything is exciting for puppies, and that sense of curiosity and fun is highly infectious. On the other hand, rearing a puppy can be hard work. They need constant attention and vigilance, and they have a lot of energy. They need to be well trained and socialized. It's very hard for a dog if the owner becomes very ill or passes away, so if you're older it may be good to consider adopting a more mature dog.

Not all adult rescue dogs have issues. Many have been lost or were handed in because their owners' circumstances changed. Often these dogs are already house-trained and have been assessed for living with children or other animals. They're so happy to have a loving home after being in kennels and repay their new owners with unstinting affection and devotion.

THE FIRST MEETING WITH YOUR NEW PUPPY

If you are buying a pedigree puppy, find out as much about the breed as possible, so that you can be sure that this breed will suit your lifestyle. When you are planning to buy a puppy from a breeder, it's vital that you see the puppies with the mother. This ensures that your pup hasn't come from a puppy farm, and you can see the environment in which your new dog has spent his first weeks. Take a list of questions, such as the age of the puppies (they shouldn't leave the litter until they're at least eight weeks old), who the father is, whether he can also be seen (though often the sire lives elsewhere), the puppies' diet (they must be weaned before leaving the mother), whether they have been checked by a veterinary surgeon, and whether they have been wormed and had their first vaccinations. The temperament of the mother is important. If she's nervous of people, this will have been transferred to her puppies. If she's friendly, this means the puppies will find it easier to bond with people. Add any other questions that you may wish to ask.

All puppies are cute, and it's easy to fall in love with them. Choose the one who feels "right" for you and, if possible, visit several times before you bring your puppy home. This enables you to get to know and bond with your pup and allows your new companion to get to know you, too. That way, it won't be quite such a wrench for him when you take him home. All family members living in your home should meet the puppy while he is at the breeder's, and if possible, careful introductions should also be made with any other dog who lives with you. You can leave behind an unwashed article of clothing, if you like, as this helps to accustom your puppy to your scent so that when you next visit he will recognize you. If you have another dog, you could rub the puppy gently with a small towel or cloth, as though drying him after a bath, and put this in your dog's bed. This will familiarize him with the puppy's scent and will make it easier for him to accept the presence of the puppy when you bring your little one home.

THE FIRST MEETING WITH YOUR NEW RESCUE DOG

Adopting a dog from a rescue shelter can be immensely rewarding. Through doing this you are saving two lives—the life of the dog you adopt and the life of another dog who can be given your dog's kennel space. The resources of shelters are always overstretched because there are more unwanted dogs than there are spaces for them, and sadly many dogs never have the opportunity to find caring homes.

You may see your prospective new dog on a rescue website, or you may visit the shelter and fall in love with him there. Shelters take in dogs of all breeds and ages, and some rescues specialize in certain breeds. One of the rescues I am involved with in the UK, Oldies Club, takes in and rehomes dogs over the age of seven. Bear in mind that you may visit a dog whose photo appeals to you, yet then discover that another dog will suit you and your lifestyle better. A reputable rescue will advise you, and you will be asked plenty of questions that should include: whether you have had a dog before; whether you work full-time or spend a great deal of time at home; whether you are prepared for the expense of adoption fees, vaccinations, possibly neutering, pet insurance, and veterinary care, as well as food and pest-control costs. You'll be encouraged to ask questions, too. Find out as much as you can about the dog—his background (if this is known), his basic temperament, how he is with children and with other dogs, and whether he has any known health or behavior issues. These factors are all important considerations in helping you make the right decision. Bear in mind that a dog's behavior in a home may be very different to behavior in a kennel situation. The dog who bounces with joy at his kennel bars may be a relaxed couch potato once he settles in with you—and the quiet, scared dog may come out of his shell and be more extroverted when he feels secure with you.

The shelter will most likely arrange for someone to visit you at home so that they can be sure your home is appropriate for one of their dogs. This usually involves checking that your garden is secure (if you have a garden), making sure everyone in the home does want a dog, and discussing your lifestyle and the type of dog who will best suit you. At this time you'll be invited to ask questions about the shelter, the adoption process, and dogs in their care who may fit in well with your family.

Usually you'll first meet your new dog at the shelter or at his foster home and will be given the opportunity to spend time with him and get to know him. Some rescues allow the dog to go home with you after the first meeting, while others may ask you to visit more than once so that you can be sure you are making the right choice. Take some treats, and perhaps a toy, so that your new dog associates your presence with good things coming his way. The move from a shelter to a home can be very stressful for some adult dogs, especially if they have lived in kennels for a long time, so getting familiar with you will make it easier for him to adjust. If you intend to visit more than once before bringing him home, you could leave an article of worn clothing in his kennel so that he is reassured by your scent.

INTRODUCING YOUR RESIDENT DOG AND NEW DOG

If you already have a dog, rescue shelters usually ask that introductions are made at the kennel or the foster home. Ideally, both dogs will be calmly introduced outside in a neutral environment. Taking them for a walk together works best. You have your dog on his leash, the rescue worker has the new dog, and you calmly walk a short distance from each other without making a fuss of either dog. Try not to let them jump all over each other or get too close at first. Just proceed on the walk, and if both dogs seem fine together, gradually draw closer to each other and allow the dogs to get introduced through some polite butt-sniffing. If all goes well and they clearly like each other, you can let them off-leash in a secure area so that they can play.

BRINGING HOME YOUR NEW DOG

Have everything ready at home before you collect your puppy or dog. He will need a comfortable bed, food and water bowls, a collar (or harness) and leash, appropriate food for his age, plenty of training treats, and some chews or toys. Ideally you will also get an ID tag engraved with your contact details to put on his collar. With older dogs you may also need worming and flea treatments. You may wish to use a crate—if so, have one ready to take with you when you collect your dog, so he can travel in it. If you have another dog, keep all chews and toys out of reach at first, so that there's less risk of conflict relating to resource guarding. Because of this, it's also best to feed your new dog and older dog separately at first, until it's clear that they have bonded. An easy way to feed the dogs separately, but in sight of each other, is to put a child safety gate in the doorway until you feel confident that there will be no conflict over food.

Before leaving to get your new dog, it's wise to check your home for anything that could harm him. Loose cables or wires need to be safely secured, cupboard doors firmly closed, any very small items that he could choke on should be placed out of reach, and precious objects that could be broken should be put away. Have fresh water in his bowl, ready for his arrival.

It can be tempting to give a new dog constant attention, and it's even more tempting if he's a puppy. Pups are so cute and cuddly that it's hard not to sweep them into your arms at every opportunity. A new dog is an exciting addition to your home and you'll want him to feel welcome and happy, but it's best to give him space to settle in and get to know you in his own time. When you arrive home, try not to overwhelm him. This is a huge lifestyle change for him, and it can be very stressful, though fortunately most dogs are highly adaptable and swiftly settle into their new surroundings.

Your new dog (and your resident dog, if you have one) is likely to pant a great deal during the first day. This is due to stress, so make sure that he knows where his bowl is and that you have plenty of water available, as panting will make him very thirsty. If you have adopted a rescue dog, be aware that he may be unused to household noises such as the washing machine, telephone, dishwasher, or vacuum cleaner and may find these scary at first. A lot of dogs, whether or not they are rescue dogs, are nervous about strange noises, especially vacuum cleaners, though some will try to grab the hose or play with it. If he seems anxious, try not to react too strongly to this, otherwise you could reinforce his fear. Speak quietly and calmly to him, and carry on with your task. He will soon learn that there's no need to be afraid of unfamiliar objects or noises.

Some dogs I have brought home have never before lived indoors. With these dogs, compassion and understanding are vital. Imagine that you have been transported to an alien planet where there are no familiar frames of reference. It would be terrifying! This is how a home can seem to some dogs who have been deprived of comfort throughout their lives. Some dogs, such as Orla, whose story you will read in part III, will immediately realize that a loving, comfortable home is the best possible place to be and will embrace life indoors with open paws. Other dogs may take a few days to adjust to the huge lifestyle change and different environment.

The first few days set the foundation for the relationship you will build with your new dog, but usually it takes around two weeks for a dog to fully relax and to unpack his baggage, especially if he is a rescue dog. I call the first two weeks the "honeymoon period" because you are busy falling in love with your dog, and he is figuring out how to bond with you and make the most of his new phase of life. Try not to expect too much from your dog—he is finding his way around and learning new rules and guidelines, and it may take him a while to catch on to some things. Being prepared for setbacks or surprises, and being understanding of the shock that moving home must be for a new dog, can help you to be patient and to deal calmly and effectively with any "teething troubles."

If you already have a dog in your home, try not to overcompensate by giving him or the new dog extra attention. Treat them the same, as much as possible. This makes it easier for the dogs to settle in together, as neither will feel that you're favoring the other.

FIRST STOP: TOILET-TRAINING

As soon as you arrive home, keep your dog on his leash for a few minutes and guide him through the home and straight into your garden. You can remove the leash in the garden, so he has the freedom to wander around. Let him sniff around, and praise and treat him immediately if he eliminates. Toilet-training a dog is easy, providing you're vigilant and are consistent about rewarding him each time he uses the preferred area. Use his name when you praise him; sound excited and happy so that he knows you're pleased with him. Let him follow you indoors and explore his new environment.

Puppies have small bladders, so they need frequent toilet breaks—I take pups outside every hour or so, as well as at the optimal times. Take your dog outside first thing in the morning and after he has eaten a meal, had a drink, or had a nap. Watch for telltale signs that he needs to "go," such as a look of concentration, sniffing, or circling. As soon as you see this, take him to his toilet area. Don't carry him—let him walk—as otherwise he won't learn the way to that area. Reward him immediately when he "goes." This is why it's important that you go outside with him. If you stand in the doorway and reward and praise him when he comes back in, he'll think the reward is for returning to you, instead of for eliminating in the right place.

You may also need to get up during the night to let him out during his first weeks with you. Remember to praise and reward him every time he goes. You can reduce the food rewards gradually, but keep up the praise.

It's hard to watch a dog every moment of the day, so some accidents may happen indoors at first. When these occur, take him outside and then come back in and clean up, without making a fuss. Avoid chastising him. A puppy can't help being a baby and having little control over his bodily functions, and a new adult dog is learning where he should and shouldn't "go." Telling him off will only make him anxious and harder to train—also, he may start to hide somewhere indoors to eliminate if he associates this with you getting angry with him.

If you can preempt him before he has an indoor accident and take him outside in time, he will be toilet-trained very quickly. Usually, with vigilance and a system of immediate rewards, this can be achieved within around three days, though some puppies and older dogs may take longer to figure out what they should be doing and where.

FEEDING

The breeder or the rescue shelter will tell you which food your new dog has been eating. It's best to carry on with this for the first few days. If you want to change his diet, do this gradually by mixing a small amount of the new food in with the usual food. You can increase the ratio a day at a time, until your dog has been completely switched over to his new diet. This helps to reduce the risk of tummy upsets that can sometimes occur when a diet is changed too suddenly, and it helps your dog become accustomed to new flavors. Aim for a diet that is free of colorings and additives, such as artificial flavorings and chemical preservatives, if possible. The healthier the diet is, the less likely your dog will become unwell, so paying a little more for his food could ultimately save you a great deal of money on future veterinary bills.

Young puppies need four small meals daily at first. This should gradually be reduced to three daily meals, and then to two meals each day from around six months. Every dog's needs are different, so be prepared to be flexible.

Adult dogs should be fed twice daily—morning and evening. Two meals a day help your dog to more effectively use the energy rush from the food, as it's distributed rather than coming all in one package. With only one meal a day, hunger makes them more likely to gulp their food and suffer from digestive upsets. Eating too fast and swallowing air can also cause gastric torsion—also known as bloat. This is a dangerous, often lethal, condition, and veterinary help should be sought immediately if your dog is trying unsuccessfully to vomit, starts pacing after eating, or is clearly in pain.

EXERCISE

Puppies should not be walked in public places until after they have had their first set of vaccinations, but they can enjoy plenty of playtimes in your home and garden. Despite their seemingly indefatigable energy, pups need only short amounts of exercise and they tend to nap a great deal. Overwalking your puppy can damage his growing joints and bones, which could cause health issues such as arthritis later on. Because of this, avoid letting your puppy jump from high places or leap in and out of your car.

Adolescent and mature dogs need adequate exercise according to their breed and level of energy. However much this is, remember to give your dog plenty of time to sniff around, so that he gains vital mental, as well as physical, stimulation.

HEALTHY LIVING

If your dog hasn't been vaccinated, wormed, or given flea deterrents, you will need to ensure that this is done as soon as possible after bringing him home. This will protect him from a number of diseases that could be detrimental to his health—and to yours! Having a microchip inserted is strongly recommended, as if he gets lost and taken to a shelter or veterinary surgery, your contact details will be on there.

Neutering or spaying is often routinely performed on rescue dogs, and if you have a puppy, your veterinary surgeon will discuss the pros and cons with you. Currently a debate is carrying on regarding this subject. One side argues that neutering or spaying eliminates the risk of testicular and mammary cancer, so should be performed unless the owner intends to use the dog for responsible breeding. The other side argues that doing this too early, if at all, can lead to behavior issues later on. Your decision will be your personal choice, based on professional advice and your own feelings.

A good diet, adequate exercise, protection from disease (where possible), and the company of caring people will set your dog up for a healthy future.

SOCIALIZING WITH OTHER DOGS

Giving your dog the opportunity to learn social skills with other dogs, as well as with people, will benefit him and will make walks or visits with friends much more enjoyable for you. Sadly, one of the reasons why some dogs end up in shelters, or awaiting a lethal injection on death row in dog pounds, is because they are lacking in social niceties. You'll find out more in the next chapter about how to teach your dog polite manners around people and other dogs, but the best time to start is when your new dog first comes to live with you.

Puppy playdates or classes are great fun for the puppies, give the owners the opportunity to make new friends and exchange information, and help to prepare your pup for a lifetime of getting along well with other dogs. Puppies learn the basics of good doggy manners during play with their littermates and interaction with the mother and any other dogs in the environment. However, these skills need to be practiced and built on, so they are remembered for life.

Classes for older dogs can be useful if you have adopted a mature dog. Some rescue dogs have had inadequate (or no) socializing, though others find it easy to accept the presence of other dogs. Even well-behaved dogs need the opportunity to interact and make friends with new dogs, so a good training class or social class, or agility class if your dog is very active, can be a real gift to your dog.

The class you choose should be geared toward the emotional, mental, and physical well-being of your dog. It's a good idea to visit without your dog first and observe a class, so that you can decide whether this is the best one for you and your dog. Ideally, classes should be small, the dogs should have adequate space between them, and there should be opportunities for play as well as learning. Only positive methods should be used. If the class teacher is recommending any methods involving force or punishment, walk away. The poor dogs in that class will most likely need behavior help in the future, through no fault of their own! Ask yourself whether the dogs and owners are obviously enjoying the class. If so, this would be a good place to take your dog.

You are responsible for ensuring that your dog, however young or old, behaves well around other dogs. It's embarrassing, and potentially dangerous, if your dog acts rudely or aggressively toward other dogs. A dog who instigates an attack is, by law, at risk of being taken from you and euthanized.

Dogs are social creatures. Given the opportunity to interact with other dogs in a safe environment, your dog will have fun, use up any excess energy through play, and will return home with a wide, tongue-lolling doggy smile and a spring in his step.

SOCIALIZING WITH PEOPLE

During the first few days, it's easier on your dog if you keep everything as low key as possible. He is learning to cope and adjust to his new environment and to you and your family. Tempting though it is to want to proudly show him off to all your friends, this can be overwhelming and nerve-wracking for him. Try to avoid having too many visitors for three or four days, if possible.

Puppies are generally very sociable and are happy to be greeted by strangers. Some adult dogs who have had unpleasant experiences in the past may find new people worrying or downright scary. Ask your visitors not to make too much fuss of your dog. Let the dog approach them in his own time, when he feels safe enough to come close. When he does approach, allow him to sniff them and ask them not to bend over him, pet him vigorously, or speak loudly to him. He will soon discover that visitors are a good thing. If he's nervous of strangers, you could suggest they throw a treat in his direction, without looking directly at him. This will help him to understand that good things happen in the presence of people who come to your home.

When you take your dog out, you can stand between him and anyone who stops to speak with you if he seems anxious. This shows him that you are protecting him and helps him to develop more confidence around strangers. Of course, your new dog may be eager to greet new people! If so, teach him good manners. Jumping up may be cute in a puppy but is certainly not appealing in a full-grown dog, and some people find bouncy dogs, however friendly, very intimidating.

ESTABLISHING ROUTINES

Dogs need a certain amount of routine and slip into it easily, as this helps them to feel secure and adds structure to their days. You can make the routines fairly flexible, as this will reduce the possibility of your dog becoming too regimented, but some dogs become anxious when their usual rituals are changed too much. For instance, if you take your dog for a walk at 8 a.m. every day, you can be sure that he'll soon expect this and possibly look expectant or start to pester you just before that time, even when on some days you may need to vary the schedule.

The main routines are those of meals and exercise. It's good to vary these slightly, but try not to make your dog wait too long past breakfast or dinner time for his meal unless this is absolutely necessary. Dogs have excellent body clocks, and when they're hungry, they can't fix themselves a snack as we do. Hungry dogs, like hungry people, can get anxious, fidgety, and antsy.

Varying the time and places for your dog's walks can give him extra stimulation and help him to open up to the enjoyment of new horizons. However, missing out on your dog's morning walk because you're too tired or busy means that a major landmark in his day has been passed, and his need for regular exercise has not been met, so it's important to play for a while or give him something to enjoy, such as a Kong, toy, or chew, instead.

Your decision to bring a new dog into your home will have been carefully thought through before you bought or adopted him. This should include considering how much time you have for fulfilling your dog's needs. If you're too busy to walk him regularly, or you're unwell, perhaps a friend, neighbor, or professional dog walker could be called on. When considering hiring a dog walker it's always best to ask for and check references. Asking friends or colleagues who they recommend is also a good way to find a good dog walker.

Your personal routine needs to be taken into account. You won't want your dog to be full of energy and eager to play just as you're about to go to sleep. You can help your dog to accept that it's time to slow down by making sure that he is kept calm and not given too much attention for an hour or so before your bedtime. A late-night game will get only him excited and leave him wanting more!

DEVELOPING TRUST

Trust, in dogs and in humans, needs to be earned. Dogs tend to give their trust easily, even when they have only known you for a short while. All they ask of us is that we're considerate of their needs and feelings and that we're consistent in our behavior toward them.

I've worked with, fostered, and adopted many dogs who have endured such terrible abuse that it seems impossible that they'll ever be able to trust humans again. Certainly people who had suffered through similar atrocities would most likely carry emotional scars for life. Yet dogs are extraordinarily forgiving creatures. Within just a few minutes of showing nonintrusive kindness, all of these cruelly treated dogs have trusted me and have healed as a result of their newfound faith that people can be kind as well as cruel. Lulu's story in chapter 3: "Body Language and Communication" illustrates this.

The primary factor in gaining the trust of your dog is to consistently treat him well. Move slowly, cloak yourself in an aura of calm, speak softly, and show him, by your responses, when he has pleased you. Avoid sudden movements if a dog is anxious or scared. Once, when Lulu was living with me, I moved suddenly and she raced into another room in a blur of black fur. A few moments later she crawled back into the room on her belly, her whole body trembling. I slowly lowered myself onto the floor and waited for her to come to me, whispering to her that she was safe with us. She crept close and lay beside me with her head in my lap, swiftly calming down as I talked to her and stroked her soft ears. This sweet soul soon learned that even a raised hand or leg no longer signaled imminent violence, but seeing her fear and distress that day brought me to tears.

Fortunately, many dogs have positive experiences of humans from an early age and so find it natural to trust everyone they meet. It's our responsibility to honor that trust and to prove ourselves fully trustworthy in return.

TEACHING HOUSE RULES

The Sympatico method stresses that only positive training is used with dogs. This doesn't mean that your dog should be allowed to do as he pleases all the time or can get away with undesirable or annoying behaviors. House rules ensure that you and your dog can live in a happy, mutually fulfilling state of harmony.

If possible, think through the important house rules that you need to get clear *before* you bring your new dog home. Try to make your list short, as this saves you from expending a great deal of time and energy instigating the rules, and it makes it far easier for your dog to learn them. The more rules you have, the more rigid the relationship with your dog becomes—and you won't want to feel like a drill sergeant instead of a companion!

I have five rules: visitors must not be knocked over as they walk through the door; aggression between dogs or growling at humans is not tolerated; begging at mealtimes or stealing food that I'm serving is a total no-no; if the couch is occupied by a dog (or dogs), room must be made for me when I want to sit there; and my dogs must come when I call them. These rules are all very easy to enforce, dogs learn them quickly and are happy to comply, and everyone enjoys home comforts without feeling put-upon. You may have different rules (perhaps you don't want your dog shedding hairs on your sofa!) and it can help to write these down and figure out which are most important to you. Whatever your rules are, consistently keeping to them is vital.

Some dogs I've worked with have to cope with so many rules that their lives are severely restricted and their owners are frazzled and frustrated through constantly trying, unsuccessfully, to enforce them. By keeping the list fairly short and making sure that you're always, always consistent, life becomes easier for all of you.

There's no point in having a rule that your dog isn't allowed on the couch and then inviting him to join you on there when you feel like some furry company. Once you make a rule, stick to it, however tempted you may feel to lapse occasionally. Otherwise this just confuses your dog and makes it likely that he'll never figure out what he can and cannot do to keep you happy.

YOU CAN TEACH AN OLD DOG NEW TRICKS!

Puppies learn quickly, but usually go through a rebellious stage when they become selectively deaf to your requests during puberty. Often at this time you need to reinforce their training. This is a natural process, similar to the way teenagers rebel in order to assert their independence. People have often told me that they wouldn't get an older dog because it's harder to teach them. This is simply not an issue—there's no age limit to a dog's ability to learn, unless he has a health condition such as canine dementia. Mature and even elderly dogs are still able to learn new things—whether these involve basic training, such as walking on a lead, sitting, or returning when called, or whether you want to teach them tricks for fun.

As well as young dogs, I've fostered and adopted dogs over the age of ten. The Shepster, who's currently with us, is fifteen. All of them learned the house rules very quickly—even those who had never lived indoors before. And all of them learned, through Skye's example, how to play and have fun with other dogs as well as with humans.

It can be very rewarding for both you and your dog if you teach him new things as he grows older. It's fun, it keeps his mind sharp, and it can add a new dimension to your relationship. You may also find that your respect for him deepens when you see just what he's capable of!

CASE HISTORY: CINDY

Cindy was a nine-week-old Cocker Spaniel, whose new owners bought her from a breeder they knew and respected. They contacted me because they wanted to make sure she settled in smoothly and easily and they were already experiencing some "teething troubles." This revealed a strong sense of responsibility toward their new puppy, and their determination to start off this new phase of their lives in the best possible way was admirable.

Although they had lived with several dogs in the past, they had never lived with a Cocker Spaniel, and Cindy would be brought up as a pet rather than a working dog. They researched the breed before choosing Cindy, but even so, her high energy and mischief levels were a shock to them at first! Cindy chewed everything in sight (and some things that were out of sight!). She barked a lot. She bounced all over everyone, sinking her sharp little teeth into arms and hands and drawing blood. And she howled through the night in her comfortable crate. However long they exercised her, through play and in their private field, Cindy's energy seemed limitless.

We devised a routine for her, as she was currently running riot. Mealtimes, exercise and play times, and rest times were drawn up on a chart and adhered to. Cindy's current exercise was too much for her age, as they were trying to tire her out. Instead of this happening, Cindy was becoming increasingly more hyper and "wired." We reduced the exercise and Cindy's owners put her in her crate, with the door open and a Kong to play with and snack from, each time she became overexcited. Because she only had her Kong while in her crate, Cindy soon viewed this as a good place to be. She became calmer indoors.

Each time Cindy started to chew something forbidden, she was called away and offered a toy or a dog chew as a distraction. Deprived of the opportunity to nibble at things that weren't allowed, Cindy soon lost interest in this and focused on her chews instead.

When she jumped up and used her teeth to grab at an arm or hand, Cindy's owners squealed loudly, detached themselves, and walked away. This taught her that nipping was not acceptable.

With the incessant barking, we solved this through holding up a hand and saying, "Enough," and then asking her to sit. Cindy was rewarded each time she sat on request, and the barking reduced and then faded away altogether, except when the doorbell rang.

Cindy's crate was in the living room, and her howling at night was due to loneliness. She had come from a litter of pups who all slept against (and on top of) each other, and it was distressing for her to sleep alone. As her owners didn't want Cindy to sleep in their room, we moved the crate to a spot in the upstairs hallway, just outside their bedroom door. This meant she could hear her owners breathing and felt comforted enough to sleep. An old sweater that smelled of her owners acted as a bedtime "snuggly" and reassured her of their presence. The howling stopped as soon as Cindy was moved upstairs. Gradually they shifted the crate further away from the bedroom door, until it was left downstairs at night. Cindy slept peacefully, and so did her owners.

Cindy grew into a model dog—sweet-natured, cooperative, and eager to absorb all aspects of her training. We were all proud of her achievements!

Chapter Nine

Training, Recall, and Those All-Important Manners

Skye and I are out walking through the fields. The sun is shining, birds are singing, and Skye happily buries his nose in clumps of grass, flanks quivering as he collects olfactory information about who and what has already passed this way.

The young Labrador appears suddenly, racing through the gap that divides two fields, and heads toward us at top speed. She's still a puppy, not more than six months old. Skye looks up and focuses, watching for body language that will reveal whether this is friend or foe. Seeing that the pup is excited, Skye dances on the spot and then trots to meet her partway. The pup prances around him, tail wagging, and Skye dances with her in a graceful waltz. One, two, three, pause for a play-bow—and repeat. I look around for the owner, and after a minute or two she appears through the gap, looking very annoyed.

"Skye," I call, and he turns and runs back to my side. The pup follows him, and I bend to stroke her and say hello. The woman shouts the pup's name in an angry tone of voice. The pup ignores her and runs in circles around Skye and me. The woman shouts again, repeatedly, as she heads toward us. She's red in the face now. I stand still so that the pup won't be tempted to run further away, and after a few more heartbeats the pup runs to her owner, who clips on her leash and gives her a stern telling-off. The pup cowers, her tail between her legs. She's just learned that returning to her owner means punishment, and this won't make recall easy for either of them in future.

All dogs need to be trained in basic manners, toileting, and good recall, and each aspect of this can be made into a fun game for both of you. A harmonious relationship with a dog who has learned the important house rules enables you to relax with him and enjoy his company. The two most important things he should learn are toilet-training and recall. So often I get called on because a dog is toileting indoors. Sometimes the owners are seriously considering giving up and taking their dog to a shelter because they can't cope with the constant cleaning up. Teaching your dog to come when you call him can save his life if he's about to run into a busy road or charge into a field of sheep or cattle. It also means that you can enjoy your walks with him, without the stress of worrying that he may take off and disappear over the horizon.

Other than toilet-training, practice the training methods in this chapter for just a few minutes at a time. Stop before your dog gets bored. You need this to be fun and rewarding for him because this will help him to pick up on the training much faster. If he's slow to figure something out, avoid getting annoyed or frustrated. Remember that he's trying to understand what you want from him, and play a fun game for a few minutes instead, then leave the training for a few hours or until the next day. You can't force learning, and dogs who feel stressed find it hard to absorb anything new.

TOILET-TRAINING

In chapter 8: "Bringing Home Your New Dog," I explain how you can start to toilet-train your dog as soon as he arrives home with you. If your dog has been clean indoors, but suddenly starts to have "accidents," it's wise to consider whether anything has changed in your situation or his environment. This could include adopting another dog; having extra people staying with you; the arrival of a new baby; or a change in your routine, such as being alone more if you have recently had to leave your home more often or for longer periods of time. If your dog has suddenly started house-soiling while you're out, perhaps something scared or unnerved him during your absence one day. Stress can cause a dog to "forget" his training, and some dogs will house-soil as a way of showing you that they're very unhappy or anxious.

If you think your dog's lapse is due to the stress of coping with change, you can find ways to alleviate his anxiety. Perhaps you could instigate more playtimes, so that he has extra fun in his life. Maybe you could put a bed in a quiet area where he can rest undisturbed if you have visitors. If you have a new baby, you can create a positive association for your dog by making sure that he has some treats or a game while the baby is in your arms.

If nothing has changed recently, ask your veterinary surgeon to check your dog, as his lapse could be due to a health problem. One dog I worked with, a very sweet Bedlington Terrier, had been constantly wetting indoors after a year of successfully remaining dry in the house, and her owners were seriously considering arranging to rehome her as they couldn't cope with the constant cleaning up. I suggested a vet check, as I suspected she had a kidney or urinary infection that was making her incontinent. They had her thoroughly examined and her urine tested, and the veterinarian diagnosed a nasty kidney infection. After a course of antibiotics, further tests to make sure there was no lasting kidney damage, and starting afresh with her training, she was soon once again dry indoors. Her owners were upset that they had come so close to rehoming their dog when she couldn't help being unwell and were very patient with her while she recovered from her illness. All manner of diseases and infections can cause your dog to lose control of his bladder or bowels, so the sooner you seek medical help, the better.

The easiest way to toilet-train your dog is to show him the area that you want him to "go" in, let him sniff around as much as possible, and reward him with praise and a special treat every time he uses his area. Do this after he has a nap, a drink, or a meal—the times when he's most likely to need to go. Watch for the warning signs of restlessness, circling, sniffing, and preparing to squat. Puppies need to go outside more frequently because their bladders are small, but adult dogs can be taken outside every two hours or so while they're still learning. After a few days you can keep up the praise, but reduce the food rewards so that he just has these occasionally. The possibility of a food reward, whether or not it appears, will prompt him to do as you ask. Stay outside with your dog, so that you can reward him immediately. He'll soon learn what's expected of him. If your dog was house-trained but has started to use your home as his toilet area, begin all over again with his toilet-training.

If your dog has an accident indoors, try to avoid reacting with annoyance or frustration. This would only make him anxious and more likely to repeat the behavior—and to hide while he does it, so that you find unpleasant surprises in unexpected places. Clean up quietly and calmly, and ignore him while you're doing this. Better still, without making a fuss, invite him outside or into another room—then wash the floor while he's away from the area. As he doesn't see you cleaning up after him, this makes it even less of an "event" and therefore doesn't become significant to him. Take him outside more frequently, and praise him fulsomely if he uses his toilet area. Dropping a treat on the ground in front of him as soon as he's finished will remind him that the reward comes for using his toilet area, not just for "going"—otherwise he may think he's doing the right thing if he "goes" on your nice new rug.

Dogs tend to choose the same areas because these hold their scent more strongly. Because of this, if he toilets indoors it's likely to be in the places where he has "been" before. Cleaning with bleach removes the scent for us, but traces of it are still detectable to your dog's sensitive nose. Instead, use a specialized product from the pet shop or your veterinarian, or dilute some biological washing powder or liquid, as this works just as well.

RECALL

It's absolutely vital that your dog learns to come to you when you call him. Dogs with poor recall may find themselves in danger through running into traffic or getting lost when they have dashed after something interesting. One dog I know was startled by a loud noise while out and took off like a rocket. Fortunately he was found a few hours later, but he ran over ten miles from his home and his lacerated paws needed a great deal of medical attention when a kind passer-by contacted his frantic owner. Some of the lost dogs handed into rescue, who are at risk of being euthanized if they're not claimed within seven days, are there simply because they hadn't been taught to return to their owners when called. This is one of the reasons why I strongly advocate having your dog microchipped, so that he can be identified and returned to you if something goes awry and he does get lost.

The best place to start recall training is indoors. What you're aiming to teach him is that good things happen when you call him to you. Once he learns this (and dogs learn very quickly), you'll find it much easier to get his attention when you want or need to. Beginning his training indoors means that he has less distractions, and you can create a fun game of hide-and-seek so that he doesn't even know that he's being trained.

Go into another room, and then call your dog in an excited tone of voice. Back this up by shaking his bag or tube of treats, and he's likely to rush to you. As soon as you see him heading for you, say, "Come," in the same excited, happy tone. You don't need to say it over and over—just once will do. Give him a treat, a pat, and lots of praise as soon as he's by your side. Keep practicing this indoors until he comes every time, then use the same game when he's out in the garden and you're indoors. Graduate to calling him when you're both outside, in different areas of the garden, and then to calling him when he seems to be absorbed in, and distracted by, something— sniffing an interesting object or cocking his head at distant sounds.

Each time he comes to you, clip his leash on for just a few moments while you praise and treat him. Then undo his leash and release him, using a command such as "Off you go!" When you do this repeatedly, your dog soon learns that having his leash put on doesn't always mean the fun is over. If you only clip his leash on when you're bringing an end to the fun and games or a walk, he'll be less keen to come back to you when he sees you have it ready!

When you know that his recall indoors and in the garden is reliable, take him to an enclosed area beyond your home, and keep practicing. Introduce interesting stimuli—another dog in the distance or children playing outside the enclosed area. Try not to get irritated if there are lapses because the distractions are more appealing to him. If he ignores you or dashes in the other direction when you call him, don't chase him—this would just make it seem more like a game to him, and he'll run further away. There are two ways to get his full attention. One is to run fast in the opposite direction, shouting happily and waving your arms in the air. He won't want to be left behind or to miss any potential fun, so he'll chase after you. The second method is to call his name, run a short way, and then drop to the ground so that you're crouching down with your back to him. He's used to seeing you upright, so will be intrigued by the sudden change on posture—and he'll come to investigate.

If his training lapses, be very careful to avoid getting annoyed with him. The owner of the young dog at the beginning of this chapter chastised her pup when she eventually did run back to her. To the puppy, this meant that returning to her owner meant she would be strongly rebuked—who would want to come back in that case? The owner was teaching her dog to associate her close proximity with punishment, and the dog was learning that her owner was angry if she came when called.

You want your dog to associate the "come" command with good things happening. This makes recall training fun and easy for both of you—you are being clear that your presence is pleasant, and your dog understands exactly what you expect of him and is happy to oblige.

At times you may find that your dog is too interested in something else to want to return to you. This is why it's best to practice in areas that are free of too many distractions until you feel confident that your dog will come as soon as he's called. Your company, especially when reinforced by treats and praise, is rewarding. However, the prospect of a roll in something horribly smelly or a game with another dog or the sight of strangers having a picnic (oh, those tempting food smells!) can prove too much to resist. The reward of your company must always prove to be greater than other rewards, so that he'll stop in his tracks as he hurtles toward the object of interest and swiftly turn to come to you instead. Always have something extra-special in your pocket or purse—a favorite squeaky toy or a treat that he only gets on high days and holidays—that you can use as backup. This will bring his attention to you, and he'll leave the other temptations behind.

EXERCISE

Use your recall training as a fun game of hide-and-seek with your dog. Hide in a different room (behind a door is good), then call him to you. Reward him each time he comes.

SIT

Teaching your dog to sit when asked is far more than just a trick. It can quickly calm down an overexcited dog and can prompt him to pay attention to you. You may want to ask your dog to sit before you put down his meal, when he starts to jump up at people, or when he's leaping around when the doorbell rings. And, of course, a dog sitting when asked is guaranteed to raise smiles and prompt praise for him from visitors!

The old method of getting a dog to sit on command is still used in dominance methods today. This involves saying, "Sit!" in a stern voice and pushing down on the dog's rear end to force his butt onto the floor. What is wrong with this? Well, firstly you should be asking nicely, as this makes your dog want to cooperate (and the Sympatico method encourages willing cooperation). Secondly, when you push down on your dog's rear, his natural impulse is to resist this and dig his heels in while he tenses and pushes back. The process becomes a battle to be won by whoever is stronger and carries more force—and this isn't the relationship you would want with your dog.

There's a much easier way to persuade your dog to place his butt on the floor when you ask him to. Choose an area of the room close to a wall, and call your dog to you. Offer him a treat. Now he's shown excellent recall and you have his full attention. Most likely he's now standing watching you, hoping you'll treat him again. Shift your position so that you're standing in front of him, with the wall behind him. Show him another treat, hold it between your thumb and forefinger, and raise your hand up and over his nose. His head will move upward along with his nose, and his body will naturally go down until he's sitting. As soon as his rear end touches the floor, calmly say, "Sit," and give him the treat and lots of praise. The reason you first practice this with a wall behind your dog is because his body has no-where to go except down—unless he shuffles sideways, in which case you withhold the treat and try again until he figures out what you want him to do. Jumping up at you to try to snatch the food doesn't work either!

After a few trial runs, move away from the wall, call him to you, and repeat the process. Dogs usually get it right very quickly and are delighted with the praise and the reward.

Some dogs will get the message so well that they'll come and sit in front of you without being asked, anticipating treats on demand. This is sneaky training (you found out all about this in chapter 6), so don't buckle to the manipulation—ask him to work for his reward by doing something else!

WATCH ME

Teaching your dog to give you his full attention is invaluable. It helps him to focus while he's learning something new, and it ensures that he concentrates on you if there are unwelcome distractions going on or if he's about to do something you don't want him to do. This is one of the first things that I teach all the rescue dogs who stay with us, and it's averted quite a few potentially sticky situations.

Kitty, a young Lurcher, had been starved and so was obsessed with food. She was also totally "wired" with excitement about being introduced to home life for the first time. During the first couple of days she bounced around like A. A. Milne's Tigger, ricocheting off the walls with delight at the prospect of food, a walk, a cuddle, and any person (new or already introduced) who came through the front door. She was tall enough to reach the kitchen worktops and joyously tried to nudge me out of the way while I prepared food. And she viewed every dog we saw on our walks as playmates and would try to drag me toward them in her eagerness to say hello. The "watch me" signal was instrumental in teaching Kitty good manners. She caught on very quickly and was soon a pleasure to be around.

Take a treat between the thumb and forefinger in each hand and let your dog see it. Now slowly raise your hands to eye level. Your dog's eyes will follow your fingers to track the treat. As soon as he glances at your eyes, say, "Watch me," and give him the treat. You can do this while he's sitting or standing.

Practice this several times a day. On the third day, don't give a treat every time you use the command. Let him figure out that it's you he needs to focus on, with or without treats. After that, use treats randomly, so that he's never sure whether he'll get a food reward or not. Always give plenty of praise, though!

You can ask him to watch you at mealtimes or if he's about to jump up at someone or is heading for your favorite shoes to nibble on them. You can also use this if he gets overexcited or reactive when other dogs or new people are around. Dogs naturally glance at us in order to decipher our moods and states of mind, so the "watch me" command taps into their desire to observe us while ensuring that we have the ability to catch their attention and redirect it when necessary.

STOP

You can teach the "stop" command if your dog barks incessantly, jumps up, delves into your trash can, or exhibits any number of undesirable behaviors. It's extraordinarily simple.

Call your dog to you. As he approaches, extend your arm at shoulder height with your hand held palm outward like a cop stopping traffic. Calmly and firmly say, "Stop." Your dog will most likely stop first time, as he'll pause to wonder why your body language has suddenly changed. As soon as he stops, praise him, step over to him, and give him a treat. Use a phrase such as "Off you go" to let him know that he can carry on about his business.

Practice this daily in different situations, so that he learns that, whatever he's doing, you want him to halt. At first he may only stop for a moment or two, so gradually extend the time so that he stays still for thirty seconds. You can make this a game, asking him to stop at random times. Remember to praise him every time, but reduce the food rewards gradually. As you'll discover in chapter 10: "Barking, Chewing, Growling, and Other Issues," the "stop" command is also very useful for eliminating the issue of constant barking.

STAY OR WAIT

Alongside recall and stopping, learning to stay in one place when asked could save your dog's life if he's in a potentially dangerous situation. It can also halt your dog in his tracks if he's about to launch himself at visitors as they come through the door. You can choose to use the word "stay" or "wait," depending on which you prefer. It's best to teach this once your dog is able to sit down on request. You can use it when your dog is lying down, too.

Ask your dog to sit. Now very, very slowly move away, backward, so that you are still facing him. Hold out your hand, palm outward, and say, "Stay" or "Wait." In the dog training world, "Stay" means the dog should remain in position until the trainer goes to fetch him, and "Wait" means to remain in place until the trainer calls the dog. As you're simply teaching your dog to keep still when asked, it doesn't matter which word you prefer to use.

If your dog gets up to follow you, stop moving and ask him to sit again. Keep him in the "stay" position for just a few moments and then call him to you for praise and a treat. Gradually lengthen the time he stays still on request, and then practice turning your back for just a few steps while you move away. You may need to be patient—if your dog keeps trying to follow you, start afresh after a break from training. After a while you'll be able to leave the room before calling him. Remember to always reward him, even if this is just praise and a pat.

Skye, and any resident dogs who are fit enough, accompany me on the walk to meet my daughter from college. At first Skye got so excited when he saw Amber walking toward us that he would leap in the air and try to rush to greet her. After two sessions of asking him to "wait" as soon as she came into view, Skye figured out that he was supposed to greet her calmly and stopped jumping around.

LEAVE IT AND TRADING

At some point all dogs acquire something you don't want them to have. Grabbing it off them or dragging them away from it creates tension and can spark off conflict. Resource guarding, where the dog acts aggressively if something is taken from him or if he is approached while guarding something, is a very common problem. Teaching your dog the "leave it" command allows you to safely remove objects from your dog and can also be used to prevent him from rolling in a smelly cow-pat, stop him from lunging at a passing dog, or stepping back from the person they're aiming to jump on. "Leave it" is a more useful command than "drop it" because you can ask him to "leave" all manner of things that aren't already in his mouth.

Teaching your dog to "trade" enables you to exchange a forbidden object for something else that will appeal to your dog, without prompting an angry reaction from him. He soon understands that when you say, "Trade," something good is about to come his way.

Start off with something that isn't really important to your dog. If he has a selection of toys, some of which he views as special and others that he takes little interest in, use the toy that provokes the least enthusiasm. Keep the other toys out of his sight for now.

Give your dog the low-interest toy first. As soon as he takes it in his mouth, place a toy that he prefers (though not his favorite one) a couple of feet away from him. He will move to take the preferred toy. As soon as he drops the low-interest toy, say, "Leave it," and offer him the preferred toy. Quickly pick up the first toy as soon as he takes the preferred toy, in such a way that he doesn't notice. Wait a minute or so, and then select another toy that he likes. Repeat the "Leave it" command as soon as he drops the previous toy. Subtly pick up the discarded toy. Don't give him the opportunity to think that you may be taking anything from him—his reward is a toy that he values more highly, so his focus will be on that. As he gets better at trading, play a game with him, in which you ask for the toy and then admire it and give it back. This way, he sees you as a "giver" rather than a "taker."

You can teach him the "trade" command using food as well as toys, and this will teach him to exchange anything in his grasp. Prepare three very small dishes—the flat plastic tops of snack tubes or cupcake holders used for baking are good for this. One should contain a few pieces of plain kibble or dry dog biscuit, the second contains a few small pieces of cheese, and the third dish has some pieces of chicken or sausage.

Wait until he seems relaxed and isn't too hungry. Just before a mealtime isn't the best time, as he'll most likely snaffle everything up fast, so teach him to trade with food midway between meals. Call him to you and place the container of kibble on the floor. Wait for him to sniff it, then place the container of cheese about two feet away, to the side. Say, "Trade," as soon as he notices the cheese and swiftly remove the kibble when he looks away from it. As he goes to the cheese (which most dogs love), let him eat the cheese and then show him the container of chicken (which most dogs love even more!). Say, "Trade," as you put the chicken about two feet away, where you had previously set down the kibble. He will then go to eat the chicken while you remove the cheese container.

Both of these commands help to ease tense situations and foster harmony. The presence of food, especially, can cause guarding issues or simply pro-voke snatch and grab incidents, even in dogs who haven't experienced pro-longed periods of hunger. This is because dogs are opportunist eaters. In the wild they never know when the next meal will come their way, so they will gorge at every opportunity. This tendency can still remain with the dogs who are our family members, unless we teach them polite manners.

WALKING ON A LEASH

So many of my clients call me because they've had enough of being dragged along while their dogs charge ahead or weave from one side to the other in front of them, pulling them over or tripping them up. It's no fun being on the other end of a leash to an excited and unruly pooch, though it may create entertainment value for witnesses! I experienced this myself once, before I qualified as a canine psychologist, when an untrained dog was so strong that he literally brought me to my knees. Leash skills are vital to the dog's safety—and to yours—as well as being an important element in the "good manners" lexicon.

If your dog pulls, drags, jaywalks, or suddenly lunges forward and sets you off-balance, it's time to teach him how to walk properly on his leash. In dominance methods, the "solution" is to jerk the leash and raise it to lift the dog's front legs above the ground. "Hanging" is damaging to the dog's tender throat area, and dogs have been known to suffer from seizures as a result.

As dogs will only do what is rewarding for them, unless they've been bullied or forced into compliance, first take a look at what could be motivating your dog to pull. Is he excited about going out, so is pulling through eagerness? Does he have enough exercise? If he has too much energy, he'll want to expend some as soon as he gets outside. Is he pulling toward things that are interesting to him, such as other dogs, people, that great-smelling tree the dogs all visit? Getting there fast, through dragging you behind him, allows him to experience the reward he seeks. Also, when the leash is taut, your dog's natural instinct is to pull harder to get away from it, so your task is to aim for a loose leash. Remember that your dog would naturally move to and fro, exploring, if off-leash, so giving him as much leeway as possible immediately reduces his urge to pull.

There are two compassionate methods you can use to train your dog to walk nicely: the stop and restart, and the bribe. Both of these ultimately reward your dog for behaving well on his leash.

With the stop and restart method, you stand still as soon as your dog starts to pull. He'll naturally stop, too, and will most likely look at you, wondering what's going on. When the leash is loose, take a step forward. If he starts to pull, stop again. This involves patience on your part because walking just a short distance may take some time. At this point your dog begins to understand that when he pulls, the fun comes to a halt and he doesn't get to go anywhere interesting. The reward for pulling no longer pays off. When he walks without pulling, he gets the reward of a good walk. Remember to praise him handsomely every time he walks nicely. You can use a word, such as "Heel" when he's close to you, and further reinforce this by giving him a treat as well as praise each time he walks by your side instead of way ahead.

The ingredients for the bribe method are a bag or pocketful of food rewards or a favorite squeaky toy that always catches your dog's attention. Hold the leash in the opposite hand to the side your dog is walking on, so that the hand nearest to him is free. Have some treats (or his toy) in your hand, just beyond his nose, and keep your fist closed around them. He'll stay near you because you have something he wants. Every time the leash is loose, say, "Heel," praise him, and give him one treat or squeak the toy. This method tends to be effective faster than the stop and restart method because he can immediately see that he'll benefit quickly. After a while he'll be so used to staying by your side that pulling on his leash will no longer occur to him.

One of the foster carers I know has a neat trick for persuading new dogs to walk beautifully to heel when she takes her group of dogs for walks. She keeps some extremely smelly liver treats in her pocket and only hands them out occasionally. The dogs never stray far from her side unless she sends them off to play!

MEALTIME MANNERS

Picture these scenes. You've spent a long time preparing a delicious meal, and it smells and looks wonderful when you serve it. Your dog sticks to you like superglue, acting as if he's been starved for months. Just as you're about to sit and eat, your dog leaps up and tries to help himself. Food gets knocked over as you try to block him from getting to the dishes. He then looms over you, drooling and pushing while you try to enjoy your meal—or he sits close beside you, gazing pleadingly at you and then your food, begging.

I've watched these scenes more times than I can count, and it's not a pretty sight. I've also experienced it briefly with some rescue dogs who have endured extreme starvation in the past. It's a guaranteed cause for loss of appetite and a forerunner for nasty bouts of indigestion, thanks to rising stress levels at mealtimes. I've also witnessed dogs leaping up to help themselves from the kitchen counter while food preparation is in progress. Yet it's easy to teach your dog that your meals are not for sharing with him.

However, you can't blame the dog for his appalling food manners. If he's a rescue dog, most likely he has gone hungry in the past. If he's grown up with you from puppyhood, you may have inadvertently taught him to harass you for food. Either way, he needs to be taught to leave you to enjoy your meals in peace.

Dominance methods insist that you eat before you feed your dog, to show him that you're the "alpha." You even pretend to take a little of your dog's food from his bowl or have a hidden snack close by so that he thinks you're eating from his bowl. This means that if your dog is hungry, he has to wait until after you've finished your meal. If you're eating later than usual, your dog will be ravenous by the time he gets his food, and he's most likely to want some of your meal. I always feed my dogs at set times, and then we can have our meal whenever I'm ready to prepare it. My dogs aren't hungry, so don't feel a sense of urgency about begging.

There are two rules to take on board when teaching your dog good manners at mealtimes. The first rule is to never, ever leave food sitting around. For many dogs this offers them temptation that's very hard to resist. The second rule is to never, ever allow your dog access to the food you're preparing or eating—this includes not feeding him tidbits from the table or if you're having a snack on the sofa. If you relent just once and let him have something you're eating, you can guarantee that, in future, he'll expect you to share—and who can blame him?

If your dog jumps up at the counter while you're preparing food, step sideways, without looking in his direction or speaking to him, so that you're blocking his access. If you give him attention he'll keep trying (attention is rewarding, remember!), so simply act as if he isn't there while you do a little side-stepping dance to prevent him from helping himself. Even the worst abused rescue dogs in my home have gotten the message before the second day is over and have never repeated the counter-surfing.

If your dog is very persistent or uses cute tricks, such as sitting and offering a paw, while you're eating, ignore him. He's using sneaky training—probably because this has worked well in the past. Eventually he'll realize there's no point in wasting his energy and will give up and find something else to do. If he barks at you, actively harasses you, or tries to help himself to your food, you'll need stronger measures.

Place his bed or a cushion several feet from your eating area. Put a chew or a treat on his bed to encourage him to lie on it. As soon as he gets up to come over to you, point to the bed and say, calmly but very firmly, "On your bed." Throw a treat onto it. As soon as he goes to his bed, say, "Bed," and praise him. This will teach him to go there when asked. At first he'll probably keep coming back to you, so repeat the instruction each time. Be patient and consistent. If you lapse just once, you'll need to start all over again with his training.

If this seems too hard, put his bed just a foot or so away from the table at first and gradually move it further away each day, a few inches at a time. Before long he'll automatically go to his bed when you sit down to eat your meal.

DOORBELL MANNERS

It's natural for your dog to bark when the doorbell rings. Quite apart from reacting to the shock of the sudden noise, this is his way of doing what he views as his job—alerting you to the presence of intruders. It's also normal (and rather nice) for your dog to want to greet visitors in a calm, friendly manner. Dogs are social creatures, after all.

Problems arise when your dog takes his role too seriously or when he gets so excited at the prospect of guests that he mugs them as they come through the door. A puppy jumping up at visitors may be cute. A large adult dog blocking your way to the door and bowling your guests over as they come in is a nuisance. This can also be very intimidating for people who are nervous of dogs, and it can have a negative effect on your social life.

You'll need a friend to practice training with you. He or she should be willing to ring the doorbell time and time again and not be allowed to enter until your dog is calm. It's best to pick a day when it's not raining or snowing for this, as you won't want your friend to be shivering for ages on the other side of your front door!

If your dog barks, but hangs back, when the doorbell rings, you can effectively use the "stop" command from the "Stop" section earlier on in this chapter. Hold out your hand, palm out like a traffic cop, and firmly say, "Stop." The moment he pauses for breath, say, "Thank you," and reward him with a treat. Ask him to sit, and reward him for sitting. You're acknowledging that you understand he's alerting you, so there's no further need for him to bark.

As soon as he's quiet, start to open the door. If he begins to bark again, immediately close the door without letting your friend come in. Repeat this until he's calm when you allow your friend to enter. Ask your friend to ignore him while you greet each other and to wait until he isn't reacting at all before calling him over to be fussed.

If your dog jumps on guests as they come in, get him to sit and stay in place while you let them in. A dog who's sitting down can't jump! Reward him for calm behavior, and remember not to let your friend into your home until he stays calm while they come through the door. You may have to practice this repeatedly for a day or two, with your friend ringing the doorbell over and over until your dog is consistently behaving well. When any guests arrive, always ask them to wait until your dog is calm before saying hello. By calling him over, instead of letting him make the first move, you're rewarding his good manners.

Some dogs are anxious about the arrival of new people in the home. If your dog runs away or hides because he's scared, ask your visitors to throw him a treat as they walk through the door, taking care to avoid looking directly at him or touching him. Don't try to encourage him to come and say hello—let him come over when he's ready. This way he'll learn that good things happen around new people, and he'll start to enjoy the prospect of company.

CASE HISTORY: DAISY

Daisy was a four-year-old Greyhound who came to stay with me soon after her racing career ended. She had only ever lived in kennels, so this was her first introduction to life in a home. Some dogs find the first few days indoors very unnerving. They've never experienced the comfort of a soft bed or the delights of wholesome food, treats, and affection. These are all viewed as wonderful, of course! But they also haven't experienced any form of house-training or the strident sounds of passing traffic, the vacuum cleaner, and the washing machine. Daisy took everything in her stride and settled in easily.

Everything was exciting and fun for this sweet, bouncy girl. Within a day she learned that the garden was the toilet area and the kitchen counters weren't for snacking from. As soon as I brought her home, I walked her through the house on her leash, straight into the backyard, and removed her leash. She obliged immediately and had treats and lots of praise. We then went indoors and she drank some water and happily explored, sniffing every available inch, before going back into the garden to play tag with Skye. As she'd had a drink, she soon needed to toilet again. She received fulsome praise and another treat. I took her outside after her meal, and each time she woke from a nap or drank some water.

Unless a dog is too infirm to negotiate stairs, all the dogs have the option to sleep in my room. This is especially useful with a new dog because I wake as soon as they start moving around to find a toilet area. Daisy woke very early the following morning, and I called her to come outside with me. This meant my floors stayed clean and dry!

On the second day Daisy knew where she was supposed to "go" and trotted happily into the garden every time. We had no accidents in the home at all.

Chapter Ten

Barking, Chewing, Growling, and Other Issues

Lulu, one of our foster dogs, barks for the first time three weeks after coming to live with us. Once she's found her voice, she goes into full cry, sounding like the Hound of the Baskervilles, every time there's the slightest noise. A cat calling in the distance, footfalls outside, passing cars—all are greeted with a cacophony of sound that brings my other dogs rushing to her in a state of high alert. Fortunately my neighbors are very tolerant. They know her sad history and always pause to say hello while Lulu hides behind my legs.

Teaching Lulu to ease up on the vocalizing takes three high-decibel days. I do this by holding up my hand, palm out, and quietly saying, "Thank you," each time she barks. After all, she's making sure to tell me that something's out there. Once she sees she has my attention (and, oh boy, she certainly has everyone's attention!), she quickly calms down. Repeating this consistently each time she starts to bark helps the message to sink in, and after the third day peace reigns for the remainder of her stay with us.

Behaviors that are normal in a puppy, such as barking, nipping, and chewing, may become abnormal if these are allowed to continue into adulthood. Puppies need to discover their voices and communicate through these as well as through body language. An overvocal adult dog is a nuisance, and I've worked with people who had been given notice to leave their homes because of complaints about their dog's barking. Puppies learn bite inhibition through nipping each other during play and discovering that the game ends if they sink their teeth in too hard. An adult dog who mouths or nips could potentially inflict a great deal of damage because his teeth are bigger and his jaws are much stronger. Puppies chew while they're teething and need to be taught which objects are appropriate for chewing and which are forbidden. Adult dogs tend to chew when they're bored, anxious, or distressed.

BARKING

A barking dog is a common cause of neighborly disputes and can even lead to litigation. Yet it's not hard to cure. Dogs bark to get our attention when they need something, such as a toilet break. They bark to alert us, or other dogs, to possible danger. Dogs bark when they're excited, especially during games like "catch." Barking can be a cry for help when a dog is distressed. They also bark because they're bored or are alone and anxious. A "Woof" when the doorbell rings is perfectly normal. Constant barking is annoying and can raise stress levels through the roof.

The first step is to figure out why your dog is barking a great deal. Is he showing signs of anxiety through other methods than barking? He may be barking because he's nervous and needs reassurance from you. In this case, a quietly spoken "It's okay" and then matter-of-factly getting on with what you were doing shows him there's no need to worry. Making a big fuss of him will reinforce the behavior and make him bark more, so walk away once you've spoken to him.

Does he think it's his job to let you know about every sound he hears or every other dog passing by? If so, hold out your hand, palm out, in the "stop" position, say, "Thank you," calmly and clearly, and leave the room. Call him from the next room, and praise him for coming to you. By then he'll have forgotten to keep on barking, and soon he'll stop the moment you give the signal.

Do you have to leave him alone for several hours at a time? Dogs often bark from boredom or loneliness. They're social creatures, and many find it hard to cope if left for long periods. Give him a Kong and a chew as you're leaving, as these will keep him occupied. You could put an old article of clothing that smells of you in his bed, as this will help to comfort him. Turning on the radio or television can help him feel less alone. If he finds it very hard to be on his own, you could even record an evening of conversation at home and play this for him when you leave him, so that he can hear your familiar voice.

NIPPING AND MOUTHING

Nipping is a minor bite, more of a nick, often caused by overexcitement. Mouthing is when your dog puts his mouth, and possibly teeth, around your hand or arm but doesn't draw blood—though it may cause bruising. A nip from a puppy who hasn't learned bite inhibition is painful and can easily draw blood. Those tiny teeth are needle sharp! A nip from an adult dog can inflict damage and may lead to a full-on bite if this behavior isn't addressed quickly. Mouthing is a way of getting attention, and so is tugging at your clothes, so your aim will be to remove that reward so the behavior stops. After all, if there's no reward, there's no point in carrying on with the behavior.

Sometimes an overexcited dog can get wound up and carried away to the point of nipping, and herding breeds such as Collies tend to use nipping at heels as a way of gathering the flock (or your family members!) together. If your dog nips, squeal loudly in a high-pitched voice and immediately walk away. If you're indoors, leave the room. You can do this if he frequently pulls at your clothes, too. If your dog puts his mouth around your hand or arm, you can either squeal and remove yourself or say a firm, "Off!" Dogs who mouth through overexcitement may get even more excited if you squeal, so use the "Off" command and remove yourself from his sight for a minute or two. It goes without saying that any game you've been playing ends immediately. If you give him a time-out of just a minute or two and then act as if the incident hasn't happened, but avoid giving him any extra attention, the behavior will stop.

CHEWING

Puppies chew when they're teething. The emergence of adult teeth is a painful process for puppies, as well as human children, and they find chewing comforting. You can save your furniture from being damaged by calling your puppy to you and offering him something that he's allowed to chew on. If you distract him and offer something appropriate each time you catch him in the act, he won't get the opportunity to gnaw through the table leg and soon he'll learn to go and find his chews instead.

Adolescent and adult dogs chew because of boredom or because they feel anxious frightened, or stressed. Chewing is comforting because it releases endorphins, feel-good chemical messages, into the bloodstream, and these help your dog to feel less stressed. As with puppies, giving your dog something that he can safely chew on will redirect his behavior. Looking into the cause is important because this will give pointers toward finding out how you can help him cope.

In adult dogs, issues such as separation anxiety often give rise to prolonged barking, chewing, destructive behavior, and house soiling.

SEPARATION ANXIETY

This is a condition that occurs because your dog feels extremely stressed and anxious when left alone. If he can't dig or chew his way out through the door or window frames to join you, he may wreck furniture or soil the house.

Some dogs can be left for several hours without trashing the home, but others find it very hard to cope for even a short while. A dog who suffers (and suffer they do!) from separation anxiety sincerely believes that he has been abandoned and will never see you again. Add to this his inability to escape to go and find you, and you may find it easier to understand your dog's extreme distress.

Owners of dogs with separation anxiety often feel guilty and try to prepare the dog for being alone. They'll make a fuss of the dog, say good-bye tenderly and apologetically, and reassure him that he won't be alone for long. All this only makes the dog's behavior worse because he grows anxious as soon as he sees the first signs that his owners are going to go out. He's likely to follow them closely, gaze pleadingly at them, whine or bark, and try to squeeze through the door with them when they leave. The heart-rending howls that follow the owners after the door has closed are guaranteed to make outings not much fun at all.

If your dog is distressed about being left alone, keep the leaving process very low key and casual. Start his training indoors, taking just a minute or two away from him. Go into another room and close the door for a moment and then come back. Avoid fussing over him before you leave and when you return. Give him a moment before you even speak to him, do something else, so that it becomes no big deal for him to see you come and go. Gradually increase the time you leave him in a room alone.

Think about your leaving ritual. Perhaps you collect your keys, phone, and purse or bag, then put on your coat before you go. Practice your leaving ritual, go through the front door without even looking at your dog, and then come straight back indoors and sit down. Pick up a book, or do something. This way, with repeated practice, your dog will start to understand that it's no big deal when you leave and that you always return.

When you do have to go out, avoid making any fuss over him. If you must speak to him, a casual "See you later" is enough. I always say good-bye to my dogs, but I don't go over to pat them before I leave because this makes the wrench of separation harder for them. Leave out some toys and a chew or Kong, and leave a radio or the television on for company. If you're going out in the evening, leave the lights on for him. Soon he will accept that you're going out but will be back, and he'll most likely spend much of his time alone sleeping.

GROWLING

Some dogs growl during play, through excitement, especially during tugging games. Other dogs make growly noises from excitement when playing chase and tag with other dogs. These forms of growling aren't issues, but it can be a good idea to stop the game if your dog's becoming too wound up.

A real growl, not related to play, says, "Back off!" If the warning isn't heeded, the dog may take things further and bite. When I work with dogs who have bitten without apparent warning, I often find that the owners have punished or chastised him for growling in the past, so the dog goes straight to the next stage instead of giving an initial verbal warning.

If your dog suddenly starts to growl at you, look to the cause. Is he in pain? A checkup with your veterinarian is always the first thing I recommend, to rule out any health conditions that could be making him feel irritable. Is he being disturbed while resting or during his meal? Sleeping dogs should be left in peace—you can't blame a dog for grumbling at being rudely awoken. Food-guarding, where a dog will attack anyone approaching his food, is a separate issue, but no dog should be disturbed while eating. With dominance methods, a dog may be deliberately provoked by having his food forcibly removed, in order to show him the human is the "alpha." This is unfair to the dog and is foolish of the person who has put him- or herself at risk of an attack.

Does your dog growl because he's on the sofa or your bed and doesn't want you (or your partner) on there? If so, it's time to redefine the boundaries and refuse to allow him on the sofa or bed. A comfortable dog bed nearby will ensure he can rest near you without the prospect of conflict over what he has learned to see as "his" area.

If your dog growls at other dogs, this could mean that he's anxious in their presence and is using his voice to tell them to go away. By turning and walking in the other direction, you remove the pressure from him and create the distance he's asking for. You can gradually introduce him to other dogs by walking him a safe distance away from them and rewarding him with treats and praise for all calm behavior. This brings about a positive association with the presence of other dogs and helps him to learn to accept that good things happen around them.

DEFIANCE

During adolescence, between around six and eighteen months of age, dogs often become unruly and defiant—rather like teenagers! It can seem as if they've forgotten the training they did so well at as puppies, and they may suddenly exhibit the irritating quality of selective hearing. At this time it's important to carry on with the training, reinforcing desirable behavior and redirecting or ignoring undesirable behavior. Sadly, many dogs are handed in to rescue shelters during the adolescent stage because they can be very hard work to be around. Patience and consistency are the keys to guiding your dog through tricky times.

When Skye was nine months old, he went through a brief phase of pushing against boundaries. Our well-behaved, cooperative puppy suddenly wanted to do as he pleased, and he displayed some impressive (sometimes entertaining, though I didn't let him see I was amused) attention-seeking behaviors. These culminated in his final act of defiance.

Beside my computer desk was Skye's favorite place to rest—a large bean-bag. I have numerous photos of puppy Skye reclining in bizarre positions on it: legs splayed out, paws in the air. One day I was working to meet a tight deadline for some magazine articles. Skye wanted me to play. I said, "Not now, Skye," which had worked beautifully up to this point. Skye stood beside his bean-bag and stared fixedly at me, trying to hypnotize me into complying. I shook my head and carried on working. He then clambered onto his bean-bag, looked me straight in the eye when I glanced around to see what he was doing—and deliberately urinated all over his favorite bed.

I immediately rose, removed the soaking wet bed to the shed in our garden, and closed the shed door. Skye's expression was of such unadulterated astonishment that I had to go into another room to laugh in private before returning to my work. The bean-bag had to be disposed of, so he lost his favorite bed—and Skye's stage of adolescent defiance instantly melted away.

RESOURCE GUARDING

Anything that has value to a dog is considered to be a resource. This may involve food, treats, toys, the sofa or your bed, that stick he found during his walk, and even people with whom he has strongly bonded. Many dogs are happy to share most things other than their most prized possessions (and some dogs will even share those). However, some dogs are extremely protective of what they consider to be theirs, and resource guarding can cause all manner of problems. It can lead to displays of serious aggression if the dog thinks the object of his affection is going to be taken from him.

It's not only dogs with deprived pasts who resource guard, though it's understandable if a dog who has gone hungry for prolonged periods feels a need to fiercely protect his food bowl. Understandable—yes; acceptable—no. Dogs who have been with their families since puppyhood do it, too, and usually this is because their owners have allowed the dog to have more privileges than are good for him. However much we love our dogs (and they're much-loved family members to many people), it's important to always remember that your dog is a dog, not a human, and that his perspective on the world is different to yours.

In looking for the solution to any behavior, it's always vital to look for the cause and for the reward that is gained through continuing the behavior. If your dog has been badly treated or starved before coming to live with you, he'll be scared that the meal you just set out for him may be the last he ever has. If your dog gets angry if you want to sit on the sofa he's so comfortable on or make space for your partner in the bed your dog's sharing with you, he considers these to be privileges that he won't give up without a battle. Whatever the reason for his behavior, the reward he gains is that you allow him to stay there and perhaps even back off so that he is the only one to have access.

In dominance methods the object being guarded is forcibly removed and the dog is chastised and "put in his place." This can set up conflict that could lead to the owner being bitten as the dog fights to retain what he views as his. The Sympatico method is more gentle and, in the long term, more effective.

In the previous chapter you discovered how to "trade" with your dog, in order to safely remove things you don't want him to have. You can use this for resource guarding concerning toys or other objects, and your dog will soon be willing to relinquish what he has when you ask him to "trade." At this point you can say, "Drop it," as he lets go of the object and reward him as soon as he does so. Before long he'll be happy to comply as soon as you ask him to drop whatever he is holding.

If your dog fiercely protects his food bowl, you can use a "passing reward" system to teach him that good things happen when you go near his bowl. However, never, ever try to remove his bowl while he is eating—after all, would you want someone to snatch away your meal while you were partway through enjoying it?

To help your dog understand that there's no need to guard his bowl, first assess your dog's comfortable area of personal space. This may be anywhere from a few inches to several feet. Avoid entering into that space until it gets to the point where your dog is relaxed and not reacting as you approach. Try not to rush him—decrease the distance at a pace that he can cope with. While he is at his bowl, pass by at a distance outside his comfort zone perimeter and throw a special piece of food (perhaps some chicken, cheese, or pieces of sausage) into his bowl as you calmly walk by without pausing. Avoid speaking to him or looking at him. Repeat this each time he goes to his bowl, so that he develops a positive association with your proximity. You'll find that he gradually becomes comfortable with your presence nearby and may even look hopefully at you as you pass.

Whether you mind or don't mind sharing your sofa or bed with your dog is your choice. Just be consistent about this. If your dog is sometimes allowed to be on there, and on other days it's forbidden, he'll be confused. If you like to have your dog beside you (personally one of life's pleasures for me is reading on the sofa beside a warm, sleepy dog), also teach him to move off the area if a person needs that space. You can do this by pointing to his bed or the floor and calmly telling him to go there. Reinforce this through putting a treat down for him, and he'll happily vacate the space in exchange for a tasty reward. After a while you'll just need to point and ask and won't need to use food rewards.

The bedroom can be the venue for competitive behavior. If you don't want your dog to go on your bed, make sure he never has the opportunity—even if this means that you keep the door closed. Your bed holds more of your scent than any other place, so it is a very appealing area for a dog.

JEALOUSY AND POSSESSIVENESS

Jealousy and possessiveness are also forms of resource guarding because the dog considers that attention, as well as desired objects, should be reserved solely for him. Reactions can vary from trying to nudge the offending person or other dog out of the way to barking, growling, threatening behavior, and even attacking whoever has the attention of his owner. This can put enormous strain on relationships if one person is being pushed out by the dog and can lead to the owner feeling forced to make a choice between their dog and their relationship.

A very common issue in dogs who have been overindulged is competition between a dog and a partner. If you have a new romantic partner, or if your long-term partner is away a great deal, your dog may respond negatively toward him or her because he's used to having the lion's share of your attention. I've witnessed dogs deliberately push the perceived "outsider" away, clamber in between people on the sofa, guard the bed to keep one person away from it, and jump up or growl at the sight of any close physical contact between partners.

What is the reward for a dog who's acting jealously? After all, you're likely to be annoyed and upset by his bad manners. The reason his behavior makes such an impact is that he does manage to get your attention and to separate you—or to at least wreck any possibility of a spontaneous romantic mood!

A dog who acts jealous or possessive needs to have the boundaries clearly redefined. Often these dogs have been allowed to get away with undesirable behavior—if one partner sleeps in the spare room, while the other shares the bed with the dog, the dog has a vested interest in keeping things as they are. He's much more comfortable in your bed, and he has the additional pleasures of your body warmth and company! Looking at what triggers his behavior, whether you have inadvertently created it, and how you respond to it will reveal how the situation can be changed for the better. Getting angry with the dog doesn't help. This only sets up more conflict, and a dog who has been allowed to behave badly will find it hard to understand why he's suddenly being told off.

The questions to ask yourself (and your partner) are these: For how long has the dog been displaying this behavior? Where does he do this? What is your reaction? Do you give in and let him create distance between you? Do you tell him off? Do you and your partner end up arguing over him? How can you bring about much-needed change?

Jealously guarding you from your partner can't be allowed to continue. Your dog isn't doing this to "dominate," but he's making sure that life remains as comfortable and affection-filled for him as it was before another person intruded on the scene. Lay down a new set of rules, and be very firm and consistent about keeping to them.

If he guards the sofa or bed, direct him onto a comfortable bed on the floor, and don't allow him to go on the sofa or bed at all—ever! You may have to block his access by putting something in front of or on the sofa for a while, until he gets the message. He may grumble a little at first (this is all very inconvenient, in his view). If so, calmly and silently remove him from the room and close the door for no more than two minutes. You're not aiming to punish him (he's done nothing wrong, as far as he's concerned), but you are aiming to show him that his behavior is unacceptable.

If he tries to stop you and your partner from sitting together or showing affection toward each other, don't separate. Just turn away from him, blocking him, each time he tries to get between you. Speaking to him or giving him any attention will reinforce his pushy behavior, so avoid doing this even if he tries every trick in his repertoire. After a while he'll realize his tactics aren't working, and he'll give up. Ask your partner to share in his care, feeding him and taking him for walks, in order to build a positive relationship between them.

Rewarding your dog as soon as he stops harassing you and your partner will reinforce the good behavior. Try not to give him too much attention at this point, as this may spark off a repetition of his previous behavior, but do acknowledge him. Praise him quietly and gently. If you wish, you can throw a treat in his direction to show him that good things happen when he leaves you in peace.

ANXIETY AND DEPRESSION

Dogs can suffer from anxiety and depression, and your veterinary surgeon will no doubt have had to prescribe medication for these conditions for some of his clients. It's upsetting to witness your dog in such a low emotional state, and he needs gentle, compassionate handling to help him start to enjoy life again.

There are a number of reasons why a dog becomes anxious or depressed. These can include a physical illness, a diet that doesn't suit him, a change in circumstances or situation, new people coming onto the scene, emotional scenes or upsets among the people in his environment, the loss of a beloved friend (human or canine), an attack by another dog, loud noises that startle him—or he may be hypersensitive by nature and find it hard to cope with anything unfamiliar.

The first step is to figure out the cause. Once you notice what triggers stress in him, you can work to alleviate this while you carefully monitor his responses. Perhaps he needs a quiet comfortable space that he can retreat to, away from noise, busyness, or overstimulation. If he's depressed, he may need to be gently guided toward activities that bring more fun into his life, in the form of different walking areas, toys, or games. The key to helping a stressed dog is to reduce the level of whatever is upsetting him and to very gradually develop his tolerance through reintroducing the triggers at a very low level and only increasing these if he seems comfortable. Learning that you will remove him from stressful situations will enable him to build his confidence in you and in himself.

Although many dogs thoroughly enjoy training classes, several dogs I have worked with found these extremely stressful. They held back from entering and cringed behind their owners. As these should be fun as well as educational for all the dogs attending them, the solution was to stop going to classes. A dog under stress is unable to learn effectively, so there's no point in forcing him to do something he finds frightening. If your dog is clearly anxious in any particular environment, ask yourself whether he really has to go there.

There are as many causes of stress in dogs as there are dogs. Sometimes you have to put your dog through something that makes him quake and quiver, such as a veterinary procedure. I've worked with several dogs who were terrified of getting into a car because they'd had bad experiences in cars in the past. At least two of these were brought into rescue after being thrown from fast-moving cars. My current foster dog, The Shepster, was so frightened at the prospect of getting into a car that he tried to bolt because he hadn't been transported anywhere for twelve years. When you have to put your dog through something that creates tremendous anxiety, be very calm, speak quietly, and try to create positive associations for him. Highly stressed dogs often aren't interested in food (could you eat if your stomach was churning with anxiety?), so it's important to find something that gives them pleasure and to take your time over getting them to where they need to be.

An extremely stressed dog is likely to need help from a qualified behaviorist who uses positive methods, and it's important to also have him checked by your veterinary surgeon to rule out a physical illness. There are products available that may help reduce your dog's level of anxiety or depression. Natural healing methods such as Bach flower remedies, which gently help to alleviate issues related to emotional and mental imbalances, can be very useful. Nutriceuticals such as Zylkene can be helpful. So can DAP collars and room sprays. Medication should be a last resort, only employed after everything possible has been done to help your dog to cope. However, sometimes medication has a place in rehabilitation when a dog is really struggling.

EXCITABILITY AND HYPERACTIVITY

All dogs get excited about some things—I'd be concerned if nothing had the power to make a dog wag his tail and light up with joy. Excitement over the prospect of a walk, a game, or being made a fuss of by visitors is normal. Too much excitement, however, can lead to your dog becoming "wired" and can cause him to act out of line. Young dogs are often easily overexcited, and if they're not taught to calm down when they get too keyed up, this can continue throughout their lives. It's lovely to arrive home to a dog who's so delighted to see you that he dances around you. It's great fun to play with your dog. But overexcited dogs can end up simply not listening to you, they can lose control and inadvertently nip you, or they can be so attracted by the dog or person on the other side of the road that they dash into traffic.

Raising your voice at an excited dog makes him more excitable, so keep your voice soft and move slowly if you use gestures or hand signals. Teaching your dog to sit when asked is invaluable. A seated dog calms down quickly because the act of leaping around only increases his feelings of excitement. Ask him to sit, reward him, and encourage him to be still for a few moments. Repeat the request if he starts to jump around again. This defuses any tension and makes him pay attention—the reward will reinforce the desired behavior and will keep his focus on you. Make sure he has a quiet retreat, such as a bed or a crate, to go to when you need him to calm down. Soon he will learn to go to his retreat as soon as you ask him to, so you'll be able to easily defuse any tension.

Hyperactive dogs are constantly on the move and find it very hard to unwind—they're like coiled-up springs that burst open at the slightest stimulus. Owners of a hyperactive dog tend to try to tire them out through very long walks and lots of play. Ironically, this only makes the dog more "wired," and the exhausted owners can't understand why their dog has so much energy after an abundance of exercise. The solution may seem strange, but it works. Reduce the exercise and playtimes, and teach your dog to learn to be calm. Have set times when your dog can express his energy, and ensure there are quiet periods during the day and in the evening when your dog is encouraged to lie quietly with a chew, Kong, or raw bone. He will receive mental stimulation from this but won't become overactive or overexcited.

JUMPING UP

Dogs jump up to get your attention, and some can be very persistent! Even small dogs can bounce pretty high (I've met Jack Russell Terriers who were like canine yo-yos, bobbing up and down so that they're level with their owner's chin), and large dogs can easily knock you off balance with a hefty leap and push. Sometimes the jumping is caused by sheer excitement, especially if you've just returned home and your dog wants to show you how happy he is to see you. Some jumping can be part of an intimidation repertoire if your dog feels he has to protect you from a visitor whom he views as an intruder—or even the passing friend you stopped to chat with while out. Watch your dog's body language to figure out whether his jumping is sheer exuberance or is a "back off" display in response to a perceived threat.

To stop your dog from jumping up, you can teach him to sit on command. Jumping and sitting are incompatible behaviors—he can't do both at the same time. Only reward him with your attention when he's sitting. If he refuses to sit, turn your back on him and either stand very still, ignoring his behavior, or walk into another room and close the door behind you for a few moments.

FEAR

Fear states can be the root cause of all manner of issues, ranging from extreme trauma (the dog who cowers behind you or tries to bolt or stays very still while they completely "shut down") to fear-aggression (the dog who viciously attacks dogs or people who come too close). Any situation or incidence that has shocked your dog could lead to fear-based issues that carry on long after the trigger incident. A sudden loud noise, an airplane flying low overhead, an attack by another dog, harsh treatment from a human—these are just a few examples of triggers.

A fearful dog may display his anxiety in a number of ways. He may become very anxious, easily spooked, overattached to his owner, obsessive-compulsive, incontinent indoors, destructive, or aggressive.

First look at what caused the original fear state. Try your best to keep him away from the source of his fear while you work on developing his confidence so that he learns to cope. Some schools of thought tell you not to reassure your dog when he's afraid. Certainly it's counterproductive to make a huge fuss of him because this will only reinforce his fear (and you're rewarding him for being fearful, so his reaction will continue). However, ignoring your dog's feelings is very lacking in compassion. A quiet "It's okay" and a light touch, rather than a stroke or cuddle, shows him that you acknowledge he's afraid and that you're in control of the situation. Be calm because then he'll pick up that you're not worried—so why should he be?

If your dog is afraid of other dogs, avoid putting him in a situation where he has to be in close proximity with them. Walk him at a comfortable distance, and reward him for all calm behavior. If he starts to look anxious or to panic, turn in the opposite direction with a matter-of-fact "Let's go." You can gradually close the distance as he gains in confidence.

If he's afraid of people, work on gaining his trust. Be aware of his interpretations of human body language. Ask people not to speak loudly, approach him, touch him, or bend over him. He'll approach them when he feels it's safe to do so. When that happens, ask them to move slowly, speak softly, and perhaps drop a treat for him, but to not look directly at him. Some dogs quickly learn to trust strangers, while others take a long time—especially if they've been abused in the past. Take things at your dog's pace because overwhelming or rushing him means that you may have to start back at the beginning.

Sometimes any sudden change in behavior, such as extreme fear, bizarre obsessions, panic states, or aggression, can be a symptom of disease, so it's always wise to have your dog checked by a vet to rule out a physical cause. One of my most heartbreaking cases was a dog who was calm when he was first adopted but who soon developed phobias about clouds, airplane trails, and indoor lights being switched on. He would try to flatten himself into the corner of the room, quaking, with his back to everyone. I asked his owners to have him thoroughly checked over as I suspected a brain tumor. Sure enough, this was his veterinarian's· diagnosis and the poor boy had to be euthanized. Fear states and other odd behaviors can also be symptomatic of conditions such as epilepsy.

AGGRESSION

Aggression in dogs is a vast subject, and if your dog is seriously aggressive, you will need help from a professional behaviorist who uses positive methods. Please avoid anyone who uses dominance methods, as these may seem like quick fixes but often lead to far worse long-term issues.

Most aggression is based on fear. A frightened dog will take one of three options—flight, freeze, or fight. If a dog cannot escape (flight) and feels too threatened to use his calming signal of staying still (freeze), he will feel forced to attack (fight). Even dogs who are trained to be aggressive, such as the so-called status dogs, are taught through being forced into situations where their only recourse is to attack.

As this is a behavior that needs careful handling and safety precautions, I don't recommend that you deal with this alone, unless you are a qualified dog trainer or behaviorist. However, ways of effectively dealing with low level aggression, such as growling or resource guarding, are described in the relevant sections in this chapter.

OBSESSIVE BEHAVIOR

Obsessive and compulsive behavior is usually stress-related. Dogs who are anxious and insecure may use obsessive-compulsive fixations in order to try to feel in control of their environment—just as people do who suffer from this distressing condition. Boredom can also be a cause. Common obsessions are balls, cats, and other dogs, but there are many bizarre objects of fixation, too. Compulsive behaviors include self-harming through constant licking or gnawing of a leg or the flank area; fly-snapping, where the dog tries to catch something no one else can see; tail-chasing that goes on and on; barking all the time, even when there's no obvious trigger; and fixating on one place and constantly feeling an urge to patrol back and forth. Some dogs become seriously ill as a result of their behavior.

You can help your dog to overcome his obsessions by using distraction methods that don't give him the opportunity to follow through on the behavior. Find something that is unrelated to his obsession, and use this to catch his attention as soon as you see him start to become fixated. Call him to you, reward him for coming, start up a game—use anything that interrupts his obsessive train of thought. If he goes back to the unwanted behavior, redirect his attention back to you.

It can take time and patience to change deep-rooted habits, so focus on the moments when you've been successful—these will give you encouragement when your dog slips back into his previous behavior. Don't expect too much, too soon, but celebrate each victory. I've worked with dogs who have been extremely obsessive-compulsive for years, and their behavior has changed within a week, simply because their owners are vigilant about watching for early warning signs and consistent about following through on distraction techniques.

PICA AND COPROPHAGIA

Pica is the term used when your dog eats weird things that may not even be edible. If your dog eats socks, stones, and other inappropriate objects, this is pica. Coprophagia is the term for feces-eating—whether your dog eats his own or other dogs' or animals'.

Both of these can be a form of obsessive behavior, and they usually get a lot of attention from the owner, which further reinforces the behavior. As with obsessions, vigilance is the key. If you can call away and distract your dog before he has the opportunity to indulge in the behavior, he will gradually lose interest in carrying on with this. Make sure you clean up immediately after him if he displays coprophagia—follow him around or keep him on his leash so that you can gently move him out of the way.

Avoid leaving objects of bizarre interest within reach if he displays pica. This reduction of opportunities contributes toward a gradual loss of interest. However, if he does manage to indulge himself before you can prevent him, don't give him attention by shouting or chastising him. If he swallows an object that could cause him harm, take him immediately to your veterinarian.

Sometimes these behaviors can arise because your dog's diet is missing something that he craves. Something as simple as changing his diet or adding some green vegetables to his food can make a difference.

WHEN TO SEEK PROFESSIONAL HELP

If you are using Sympatico methods and your dog's behavior continues, with no change, for more than a week, it's best to seek professional help. Have your dog checked over by your veterinarian in case any health issues are the cause. Call in a behaviorist or trainer who uses positive methods if your veterinarian pronounces your dog healthy. Owners often feel embarrassed or guilty about their dog's undesirable behavior—but sometimes just speaking with a professional can give you the confidence to keep on working with your dog. It can help to write down the times and places where the behavior occurs, in case a pattern emerges. It also helps to look at the positive changes that occur because these boost you and help you to keep going when you're having a tough day or if you feel discouraged. Ultimately, you want the best for your dog, and he wants to do his best, too. Gentle guidance will help you to overcome issues and will strengthen the bond between you.

CASE HISTORY: FREDDIE

Freddie is an adorable middle-aged Springer Spaniel who was brought to me because his barking was such a problem that he was handed into a rescue shelter. He had been a barker since youth, and his two previous owners both had problems with complaints from neighbors and ear-splitting headaches from the constant noise.

Freddie trotted happily into my home and introduced himself politely to my dogs. He was eager to make friends with the people, too. Then a car drove by. Freddie barked. And barked. And barked. He paused for breath just as Amber, my daughter, walked through the room, and her presence set him off again. His fosterer looked at me and raised her eyebrows. My dogs looked at me in amazement. Freddie was loud! I waited for him to stop for just a moment to catch his breath, raised my hand in the "stop" position, said, "Thank you," and gave him a treat. Freddie looked pleased and surprised— and he couldn't bark while he was chewing.

Amber walked back through, and Freddie started barking again. I raised my hand and said, "Thank you." Freddie stopped and ate his treat. This was repeated numerous times. After two hours Freddie was peacefully and silently lying on my feet, while his fosterer and I sat on the sofa, drinking cups of tea and chatting. A while later he started to bark again, so his fosterer took over—after all, she had to live with him! It worked, and that gave her confidence.

Freddie really just wanted attention and acknowledgment. Everything he heard and saw had been highly stimulating for him, and he wanted to make sure everyone knew he'd noticed. By simply thanking him and rewarding him for silence, he had no need to keep alerting everyone. His fosterer carried on with his training at home, and soon Freddie was calm and quiet enough to be put forward for rehoming. He was adopted and has settled in beautifully with his forever family.

Chapter Eleven

The Games People (And Dogs) Play

During the first few days of Skye's new life with us, he learns the name we have given him. We frequently call him out into the garden to tumble, bear-cub-like, through the plants and over the small rockery. He quickly learns that an excited call of "Skye!" means a treat, a pat, and a game, and he comes running, high-stepping like a tiny racehorse. While he's outside he eliminates, so he learns toilet-training and recall at the same time—without even realizing that he's being trained. Amber and I get to have fun teaching him, and our home is constantly filled with the sound of laughter. There are few things more entertaining than a puppy who's keen to sample all the delights that life offers.

Sharing your life with a dog (or dogs) should be fun. Teaching good manners and training your dog to pay attention to you work even more effectively when you do this through play. Like children, dogs can remind us to not take life quite so seriously—and they make such great playmates! There's something about the purity, the innocence, the waggy-tailed enthusiasm, and the sheer unadulterated curiosity of a dog that has the power to open our hearts and make us smile.

The games in this chapter can include all members of your family, and they help your dog to learn while you're all having a great time. Some, such as the "cup game," have been used by research scientists in order to figure out how much of our body language dogs understand. Others, such as "Find the treats" employ your dog's natural abilities and give him the opportunity to (literally) nose out rewards. And some, such as "Tidy your toys," are fun for him to play while also giving him a task to accomplish that helps you, too!

You'll notice that food rewards are used in these games. If you distribute these from his daily allowance of food, you won't need to be concerned that he may put on weight. It can be tempting to let your dog engage in rough play, so try to avoid letting him become too overexcited. If you let him grab at your clothes and your arms or snatch a tug toy, you'll then have the additional task of teaching not to do that! Some dogs love rough-and-tumble play, while it can be intimidating for others, so if you do let a little rough play creep into some of your games, observe your dog's reactions to this.

NAME GAMES AND RECALL

Unless your dog has been adopted with a given name from his previous owner, he's unlikely to know his name when he first comes to live with you. Your puppy may be given a name by the breeder, but you can change this to one of your choice when you bring him home. If you have adopted a rescue dog, the shelter may not know his name and so will give one to him. Again, you can change this if you prefer, though it's easier on your dog if you start to use your chosen name for him as soon as you collect him.

Use his name whenever you speak to him, and keep your voice light and cheerful. Reward him for looking up or coming over to you when you call his name because this creates a positive association between his name and good things happening. He'll quickly learn that you're asking him to pay attention to you and will start to come when you call him. Soon you'll be able to call him from another room and he'll respond.

If you need to stop him from doing something he really shouldn't be doing, avoid using his name. Say, "Ah ah" or "Oh oh," while shaking your head instead. If you use his name when ticking him off, he won't feel motivated to come to you when you use it for anything good.

Like my daughter and me in the little anecdote about Skye at the beginning of this chapter, you can call your dog out into the garden so that he learns toilet-training easily. You can call him into the kitchen at mealtimes, or call him into another room for a game with some toys. The bond between you and your dog will grow stronger, and he will learn all-important recall.

HIDE-AND-SEEK

Once your dog knows his name, you can further develop his recall skills through playing hide-and-seek with him. Go into another room and call him. As soon as he finds you, reward him with praise and a treat. When he regularly comes running when called, add more interest to the game by hiding out in the garden or indoors behind a door or behind the sofa. Call his name, and as soon as you hear him coming to find you, stay quiet for a few moments. If he seems to be veering in the wrong direction, call him again.

Your dog will soon start to track you by your scent as well as your voice, so you won't need to call him repeatedly—just occasionally will let him know you want him to find you. As soon as he does, make sure to reward him!

This game can prove very useful if you're out walking and your dog moves out of sight, as he's already learned to follow the sound of your voice.

THE CUP GAME

This was used in experiments by Dr. Brian Hare, primatologist at Duke University, and has also been used by other scientists. The purpose of the original experiments in cognition was to determine whether dogs can figure out what a human is thinking—but this is a fun game for you and your dog to play, too.

Set out three cups, laying them face-down. Call your dog to you, show him a treat, then let him see you place the treat beneath one of the cups. Point your forefinger to the cup the treat is hidden beneath, and tell him to get the treat. He'll be watching you, and the aim of the game is that he'll follow your pointing finger and knock the cup over to get the reward. If he doesn't "get it" straight away, be patient. Push the cups over for him, so that he can see what he's supposed to be doing.

You can play variations on this game when he figures out what's expected of him. When he's skilled at following the direction of your finger, try just using your eyes to look hard at the cup containing the treat. Once he's mastered this, you can try glancing swiftly at the cup, then at him. Graduate to putting the treat beneath a cup without letting him see where it is—and let him find it.

This game teaches your dog to watch you closely. From an early age, most dogs will follow the direction of a pointing finger and an aimed glance. Playing the cup game is a great way to encourage your dog to focus on you.

DROP IT

This game is immensely useful training for those times in the future when you want your dog to relinquish something without him feeling challenged or threatened. Start the game with a fluffy toy or a ball, and always make sure you have a substitute for this hidden behind your back.

Offer your dog the toy, and let him play with it for a minute or two. Then bring out the hidden toy and offer it to him. As soon as he drops the toy in his mouth, say, "Drop it," and give him the second toy. Hide the first toy behind your back for a minute while he plays with the second toy, then repeat the process. You can gradually move on to playing this game with dog chews— but it's very important that you always have a substitute reward that is as appealing, or more desirable, than the one you are asking him to let go of.

When he's learned this, and is reliable at dropping the object in his mouth, you can play the game from a distance of several feet—throwing the first toy to him, then calling him over to you and asking him to drop it at your feet or directly into your hand.

The method you use in the "Drop it" game can also be used in a similar way to teach him how to "trade" and "leave it," which are explained in chapter 9: "Training, Recall, and Those All-Important Manners."

FIND THE TREATS

All dogs have a far better sense of smell than we do, and the noses of the tracking breeds are even more sophisticated than those of their fellow canines. Playing tracking games such as "Find the treat" are great fun for your dog, and they stimulate him both mentally and physically. And it can be illuminating for you to see just how clever your dog is at finding hidden goodies!

Start off indoors in a fairly small space. If he's in the room with you when you prepare, ask him to sit or lie down, otherwise he'll snaffle the treats before you can set them out. Lay a thin trail of small treats that lead to a chair or sofa, and place a larger treat beneath the furniture in such a way that it's hidden but he can get to it. Once you're ready, point to the first treat and tell him to go get it. He'll follow the trail and hopefully also find the hidden reward. Do this once a day for a couple of days, and see how his speed picks up!

From here, you can play the game out in the garden or yard. Hide the final treat behind something so that he can't see it, and let him follow the trail. This tracking game can lead to a toy instead of a food reward.

OBSTACLE COURSE

Active dogs thoroughly enjoy the challenge of an obstacle course. You can set up your own in your garden or even indoors if you have enough space for him to easily move around. He has to figure out what you want from him and also work out ways through and around obstacles, so this game is great for providing him with extra exercise and mental stimulation and for strengthening his bond with you.

Set out a collection of objects you can use as obstacles. These could include anything you like, so long as it isn't potentially harmful to him. Dining chairs and small piles of books or cartons for him to twist and turn around, pillows that he can jump over, an old cloth draped between two chairs to create a small tunnel, even a couch that he can leap on and off (if you have enough play space) are just some of the possibilities. Place these around the designated area to create a course that he will have fun negotiating. Ideally these will provide things that he can maneuver around, jump on, and jump over. One of my friends had the brilliant idea of using a children's play tunnel as part of her obstacle course.

Before you start the game, show him that you have a treat in your hand. Hold the treat so that he can see it but can't take it from you until you unfurl your fingers. Letting him keep his focus on the treat, slowly weave your way around the obstacle course—he'll most likely follow you closely! Use the hand holding the treat to direct him around, so that he can literally follow his nose as he moves with you. Give him the treat at the end—or even partway round the course if you like, though if you do this you'll need to carry on with a fresh treat in your hand. Give him lots of praise and encouragement in an excited, happy tone of voice as you go along. You could even ask someone to video you and your dog, so that when you watch it you can see which areas he most enjoys.

As he becomes more skillful, you can reduce the food rewards, and simply direct him with the hand that previously held the treats, though he should always have a reward when he finishes the course. Experiment with obstacles. Out-of-doors you can direct him around trees or bushes and over low fences.

FOLLOW THE LEADER

In the obstacle course game, your dog learns to follow your directions while observing you closely. You can also have fun playing "follow the leader" by calling your dog and encouraging him to follow your hand that holds the treat. Change direction frequently, twist and turn, and praise and reward him for staying close behind you.

This game can be useful when you're teaching him to walk nicely on a loose leash. Start indoors, without putting his leash on, and then play the game in your garden or any safe enclosed outdoor space. If you clip his leash on after he's learned to stay close to you, you'll find that he hardly notices he's on-leash and won't think to pull away. Be sure to keep the leash very relaxed and loose, as any tautness on it will make him instinctively want to pull away from you.

FETCH

In order to fetch and deliver a toy to you, your dog has to first go after it, then pick it up, then bring it back to you. Retrieving breeds learn this easily, but some other breeds can take a while to catch on.

To play the "fetch" game, put several toys and some treats in your pockets or a bag. Throw a toy a short distance, point to it, and excitedly encourage your dog to run after it. Use a phrase that will be his signal in future, such as "Go get it!" Your dog is likely to pick up on your enthusiasm and dash after the toy. When he picks it up, call him to you, saying, "Fetch" or "Bring" as he comes toward you. If he picks it up, but runs away from you, turn and run in the opposite direction to get him to follow you.

Praise and pat your dog as soon as he comes close. Offer a treat or another toy. He'll drop the one in his mouth so that he can take what you're offering—similarly to when you teach him to "trade." Soon he'll be happily retrieving objects and dropping them in your hand.

TIDY YOUR TOYS

This game is fun for your dog, and it can be very useful for you to have some canine help around the house!

Have a box or basket of toys nearby and some treats in your pocket. Empty the toys out and let him choose one that he wants to play with. Have a game with him, and then offer him a treat. As soon as he drops his toy, point to the toy box, pick up his toy and place it the box, and say, "Tidy up," in a happy tone of voice. Offer him another toy. When he picks up the toy, point to the box and say, "Tidy up." Reward him with a treat and another toy as soon as he does as you ask.

It may take him a few attempts to figure out exactly what you want him to do, but once he's got the message, he'll enjoy being your helper!

EXERCISE

Pick out one of the above games, and play it with your dog at least three times. Observe his reactions as he figures out what he's supposed to be doing and his pleasure when he gets it right.

CASE HISTORY: SKYE LEARNS TO CATCH

Skye was never interested in the television as a puppy—he still mostly ignores it if it's on—but on one occasion he sat up, paid attention to it, and learned a new game.

He was around six months old at the time and had grown too tall to be able to easily fit on my lap. I was sitting on the sofa, watching the televised Crufts dog show, and Skye was stretched out beside me with his head and shoulders in my lap, dozing. Then a demonstration of Collies playing Flyball appeared on the screen. This involves two teams of dogs who race each other over obstacles to catch a ball and return with it. The next dog in the team can only move forward when the dog before him has returned with his ball. It's fast and very exciting to watch.

Skye woke up. He heard the cheers coming from the television and glanced over at it—then jumped off the sofa and sat right in front of the television, watching closely. In this particular demonstration a man was standing on a podium to throw a ball in the air as each dog approached. The dogs leaped up to catch the ball and leaped over hurdles to return to their teams. Skye seemed to be entranced at the sight.

One of our evening games was always a ball game. I'd throw the ball, and Skye would run after it, pick it up from where it had landed, and bring it back to drop it at my feet or in my hand. That evening the game changed. I threw the ball, expecting Skye to turn and run after it, but he changed tactics. He leaped in the air just as the ball was sailing over his head, caught it in his mouth, and proudly trotted over to drop it in my hand.

Years later, Skye still loves this game best of all!

III

A Meeting of Hearts: Thirteen Success Stories

Chapter Twelve

Success Stories

HECTOR: BARKING THROUGH THE NIGHT

Hector, a very cute four-month-old Cocker Spaniel puppy, was driving Sarah, his owner, to distraction. He was very needy, and Sarah was in tears of exhaustion because he was barking most of the night. Sarah and her neighbors were hardly getting any sleep, and the situation had reached a crisis point. If Hector didn't ease up soon, Sarah told me, he would have to be rehomed.

Sarah had bought Hector from a breeder and brought him home when he was eight weeks old. He had cried and barked through the night right from the start, so it was astonishing that Sarah had coped for so long on very little sleep. Hector barked very little during the day and napped after his daytime walks, but Sarah worked full-time from her office at home and needed to stay awake. Naps for her were out of the question and wouldn't have resolved his nighttime barking. Fortunately a checkup at the veterinarian's surgery showed there were no health problems, and his diet was good, so the issue wasn't related to any illness.

Observing them together, it was clear that Hector was very dependent on Sarah. He followed her every time she got up from her chair—even when he seemed to be sleeping, his eyes opened the moment she moved. He looked at her frequently, as though checking that he had her approval, and was happy to simply be by her side. Apart from her frustration over the rough nights, they had a mutually loving relationship.

There was no doubt in my mind that Hector's barking problem was caused by loneliness. He had spent his first weeks with his mother and littermates, where he was never alone, and it was scary for him to be in a room all by himself. Dogs are very social creatures, and when clients are planning to get a new dog, I usually suggest that they spend the first couple of nights sleeping in the same room as their dog. If they don't want the dog in their bedroom, one person could sleep on the sofa or a camp bed in the living room with the new arrival for the first couple of nights. This eases the shock and distress of change and helps the dog settle in more quickly and easily. Hector still hadn't figured out that Sarah would return after leaving him at night, so we needed to slowly and compassionately get him used to spending nights on his own.

Sarah didn't want him to sleep in her bedroom because she felt strongly that this was her private space. An easy solution would have been to let Hector sleep in her room, but as this wasn't an option I suggested she temporarily modify the sleeping arrangements. Sarah would put a child safety gate at her bedroom door so that Hector couldn't enter, and she would leave the door ajar and place Hector's bed just outside her room. This way he would know that she was close by, and he could smell and hear her. This would reassure him.

The bedtime routine needed to be very low key. Saying a prolonged good night to Hector, cuddling him and apologizing for leaving him, was only making him aware that he was about to be left alone—and this increased his anxiety. A matter-of-fact good night and a stroke of his head was preferable to a long good-bye.

Sarah was willing to do this, so started the new bedtime routine the same night. She called me the next day, absolutely delighted, to say that Hector had only barked once during the night and that a quiet "Shhh" from her had assured him she was close by. He had quickly gone back to sleep.

As Sarah wanted Hector to learn to cope with sleeping downstairs, I encouraged her to move Hector's bed a few inches farther away from her bedroom door each night. This would help him to gradually get used to being some distance from her. One night she moved him too far away, too quickly. He cried and barked, so she moved him just a little closer, but not right beside her bedroom door. Within two weeks Hector was happily sleeping in the living room and there had been no more nighttime barking.

JOEY: OBSESSIVE-COMPULSIVE DISORDER

Obsessive-Compulsive Disorder (OCD) is as common in dogs as in humans, and the way in which this manifests is just as varied. Some breeds are known to display specific forms of OCD, such as flank-licking in Doberman Pinschers, and the severity of the disorder can range from a mild irritant to a serious health risk.

Joey, an elderly Yorkshire Terrier, had lived with his owners, Sue and John, since puppyhood and had always shown obsessive tendencies. They asked for my help because they had tried every other available possibility, without success, and his OCD was affecting his already frail health. Joey was spending every waking moment patrolling back and forth beside the garden fence, simply because occasionally he had seen the neighbor's cats on the other side. He couldn't rest or relax, and he had no inclination to play with his owners in his lovely garden.

The most effective way to eliminate obsessions and compulsions is to give the dog no further opportunity to follow through on these. As Joey had suffered from OCD throughout his life, I told Sue and John that it may take some time and a great deal of patience and vigilance to help Joey through this. His caring owners were happy to carry out my advice, no matter how long it took to change Joey's behavior. Fortunately, Joey responded so well that it took just days, rather than the weeks that we had anticipated, for him to stay away from the fence.

The main aim was to distract Joey every time he started to focus on or move toward the fence. Sue and John started Joey's new training indoors, first of all, so that he couldn't become fixated while outside. Each time they went into a different room, they called Joey in a happy tone of voice. He came running to them each time and was rewarded with lots of praise and a treat. When they went into the garden, they called him again, kept his focus on them by showing the reward in their hands, and then went straight back indoors and called him to follow. Joey was a bright little dog and thoroughly enjoyed this new game and all the extra attention it brought!

Because Joey's owners felt there was now an action plan that could work, their confidence increased. Of course Joey sensed this and so was even happier to do as they asked. OCD often stems from stress and a feeling of not being in control, and Joey's owners were kindly and compassionately making it clear they were in charge. This reassured Joey, especially as he had clearly been "picking up" on their anxiety about him.

Each time Joey went outside and started to move toward the fence, Sue and John called him indoors. They did this repeatedly during the first two days. On the third day, Sue phoned me to say that Joey was playing in the garden with them and hadn't even looked at the fence! We were all delighted that he had "got it" so quickly.

During the first week, Joey had just a few occasional lapses and headed for the fence to pace. Each time, his owners called him straight back indoors. By the second week, Joey could go out in the garden alone, with no sign of taking an interest in the fence. I'd warned Sue and John that sometimes a dog with severe OCD will redirect it onto another area of obsessive interest, so they were prepared for this. However, Joey responded so well to his new training that he remained happy and stable until he passed away.

SAFFY: EARLY MORNING BARKING

Being woken by a barking dog is no fun, and to have this happen very early every morning can stretch your patience and tolerance to the limit. When the dog is a two-year-old Basset Hound, short in stature but big in voice, it's the worst way to start the day.

Basset Hounds are very sweet dogs and their worried-looking faces are immensely appealing. You just want to make them feel happy—and this is exactly what was causing the problems for Saffy's owner, Anna! Saffy only had to look at her owner with her sad eyes or give a deep woof, and Anna leaped to comply with whatever she wanted. Fortunately, Saffy wasn't a demanding dog. She thoroughly enjoyed her walks, her meals, and her evenings spent snoozing at Anna's feet. Her only issue was that she expected Anna to rise and serve breakfast at 4 a.m., and she made sure that Anna couldn't sleep any later. Even earplugs didn't shut out Saffy's deep, resonant barking, and the neighbors were none too happy by the time Anna contacted me.

Observing them together, I could see that they shared a beautiful affectionate bond. I could also see that Anna constantly tried to preempt Saffy's needs and wishes and that, because of this, Saffy had received no training in coping with delays or frustration. Most dogs experience this naturally during puppyhood, when they have to compete or wait their turn to suckle from the mother and when they clamber over each other to nudge littermates out of the way. Saffy's every need was being met before she even realized the need was there! This meant that when she did want something—company and breakfast—she expected it to be delivered immediately.

We discussed Saffy's routine and mealtimes. Her evening meal was at 5 p.m., so I suggested this be moved back an hour to 6 p.m. for a while. There was no reason for Saffy to be hungry at 4 a.m. as her diet was very healthy, but a slight change in food routines would contribute to helping her break the pattern of barking for breakfast. As Anna had always stumbled downstairs at 4 a.m. to feed Saffy on demand, we agreed on a new morning routine. The next morning, Anna would come downstairs and open the door so that Saffy could go into the garden to eliminate, but would give her no attention whatsoever—not even a "Good morning" pat. Anna would then make herself a drink and go back upstairs for ten minutes, ignoring Saffy if she barked. When she came back down, she would calmly greet Saffy as soon as she stopped barking, do something else for a few minutes, and then fix breakfast for both of them. On each consecutive morning, breakfast would be served a little later.

On the first morning Saffy was so perplexed by this change of routine that she stood in front of Anna and barked directly at her. Anna turned away and only gave Saffy attention when she quieted down. On the second morning Saffy barked until Anna rose but quieted down when she had opened the back door and retreated upstairs. On the third morning, Saffy gave just a short "Woof." Anna repeated her new routine. Within a week Saffy was sleeping until 6 a.m., a far more acceptable time for her owner and the neighbors, and woke Anna with a low-decibel bark!

If Anna had wanted to delay her rising time a little longer, she could have done this, but she was happy to rise at 6 a.m. and felt that Saffy's training had been hugely successful.

CINDY: DEPRESSION OVER A NEW BABY

Cindy, a tiny twelve-year-old Toy Poodle, had lived with her owner, Layla, since the age of eight weeks. Throughout her life Cindy had been Layla's "baby." She accompanied her everywhere, rested on Layla's lap when she sat down, and slept on her bed. Her problems started when Layla married and had a baby, who was nine months old when I was called in to help.

The change of situation had been enormously stressful for Cindy, who had no problems sharing Layla with her husband but clearly felt the baby had usurped her place in Layla's affections. Layla had tried to compensate for this by giving Cindy extra attention whenever she looked sad and when the baby was asleep, but Cindy sank into a state of depression and seemed to lose interest in everything. She showed no antagonism toward the baby and chose to completely ignore her instead. Presumably she hoped the baby would go away at some point, but as she was still having to share Layla nine months later, the little dog was making her unhappiness very apparent.

Cindy had been refusing her food for some time and had lost a great deal of weight. In desperation, Layla left food down for her at all times, in the hope that she would snack through the day. She also hand-fed Cindy small morsels from her plate, and this was all she would eat. Where she had always enjoyed her walks, though she was nervous of being approached by strange dogs, Cindy now refused to walk at all. Layla tried repeatedly to coax her out on her leash, but Cindy simply lay down and refused to move until Layla carried her. A thorough checkup at the veterinarian's, including blood tests, showed no abnormalities, and the veterinarian suggested antidepressant medication, which Layla felt wasn't the answer. Cindy's issues needed to be dealt with, not masked, she told me.

I asked Layla when she played with Cindy, and Layla told me that she initiated playtime when the baby was asleep, so that Cindy could have one-to-one attention. This was reinforcing Cindy's feelings that the baby was a competitor.

We set up a new regime. Cindy was being given extra attention for looking sad, so this was reinforcing her behavior. From now on, Cindy would receive extra attention and lots of praise every time she looked alert or took notice of what was going on around her.

As Cindy was now very underweight and her stomach had shrunk, she would have four very small meals each day for a while. Too much food on her plate would most likely put her off eating altogether, so these additional meals would provide the nourishment she needed without seeming too much for Cindy to cope with. As Cindy preferred chicken, Layla made small quantities of chicken mixed with rice and vegetables and portioned this out through the day. I asked her to stop feeding Cindy from her plate. This is never a good idea, and it was making Cindy's eating habits even worse. Instead, she served Cindy's meal at the same time as she had a meal or small snack and put the dish on the floor beside her. As Cindy's appetite increased, Layla would gradually move the food bowl farther away and reduce the number of meals while gradually increasing the quantities given at each meal. The food bowls were to be removed after thirty minutes, even if Cindy hadn't eaten anything.

From now on, Cindy would have extra attention and playtimes when the baby was awake and with Layla. This would help Cindy to realize that the presence of the baby meant good things would happen, and this would encourage her to think of the baby as a member of her social group, instead of as an intruder who had taken over Layla's affections.

Encouraging Cindy to take some exercise would strengthen her muscles and increase her appetite—and her sense of well-being. Layla would take her outside for just five minutes and call Cindy to walk beside her in an upbeat tone of voice. If Cindy sat or lay down and refused to move, Layla would simply wait, without making a fuss or picking her up, and then turn to walk back home. This worked well, so the time outside was increased by a few minutes daily until Cindy was enjoying twenty-minute walks with her owner.

Within two weeks, Cindy seemed like a different dog. She was alert and playful and seemed much happier when the baby was awake. She was eating better and had put on a little weight, so she was having three meals daily instead of four. This would be further reduced to two meals after another two weeks. She was enjoying her walks to the extent of getting up as soon as Layla picked up her leash. Poodles are highly intelligent dogs, and Cindy had quickly learned that being cheerful instead of looking miserable paid off far more in terms of attention and rewards.

A month later it was hard to believe that Cindy had ever had issues!

SNOWY: DISRUPTIVE BEHAVIOR

Snowy's owner was on the verge of rehoming him when she called me. Her year-old Bichon Frise boy was disruptive in the extreme. He jumped up at everyone, including her two children. He stole food and toys and refused to give them back. He toileted indoors, he had torn apart several dog beds, and he was now confined to living in the kitchen.

When I visited the home, Barbara, Snowy's owner, warned me to steel myself as I walked through the door and we headed toward the kitchen. A child safety gate was already in place so that Snowy couldn't escape. As I approached, I looked at this little white dog bouncing up and down like a yo-yo and could see no signs of aggression whatsoever. He was just a very overexcited adolescent. And, as the kitchen floor was bare of all but a duvet, he was also an extremely bored adolescent, which is a recipe for disaster!

I climbed over the gate and went to join Snowy. He jumped up repeatedly. I turned my back on him and crossed my arms across my chest without saying a word, shifting my body each time he tried to come around to my front. His claws were sharp, but he kept his teeth in his mouth, and he was yipping with glee about the unexpected company. After a few minutes of Snowy leaping about and his owner telling me this was how he behaved all the time, the little dog stopped, sat down, and looked at me with a puzzled expression. He was used to being shouted at and batted away. "Hello, Snowy," I said quietly. Snowy started jumping again. I turned my back on him. He sat down and waited. This little pas de deux went on for about ten minutes, until Snowy was calm enough that I could sit on the floor beside him. He immediately climbed onto my lap, his tail wagging as he made himself comfortable. Barbara looked astonished.

I suggested we let Snowy out of the kitchen, so that I could see how he behaved. We went into the living room, Snowy following, and sat down. The children were sitting on the floor with a snack bar each, watching television. Snowy immediately dashed to the nearest child and tried to take her snack bar. The little girl raised it above her head, looking panicked. I called Snowy, and he came straight over to me. He got a treat and lots of praise and settled down beside me on the sofa. This wasn't the devil dog I'd been expecting to meet!

The children gathered together a few toys, so that I could see Snowy's reaction. Immediately he pounced on one and carried it off with his tail held high. I called him to me. He did a little dance but came after a few moments. As soon as he was close, I offered a treat. He immediately dropped the toy to take the reward, and I said, "Trade," and gave the toy back to the child. I expected Snowy to go after it, but he sat in front of me and unconsciously lifted a paw. This was an immensely trainable little dog!

During the several hours that I spent there, Snowy responded quickly to every instruction. I pointed out how bored he must be. Imagine living in a small, empty space, with nothing to do all day—it would make anyone destructive! As the kitchen door was left open, Snowy was expected to take himself outside and still hadn't figured out toilet-training. We all went for a walk together, and Snowy thoroughly enjoyed having a good sniff around. Barbara told me she had been too busy to walk him for more than ten minutes a day, which wasn't enough for a young dog with a lot of energy to burn.

Back at the home, we talked through Snowy's new training, and I wrote down instructions that Barbara posted up on the kitchen notice board. The children would also be involved in this.

Snowy would be properly toilet-trained. Barbara and the children would make sure that someone went outside with Snowy after each nap, drink, and meal. They would also take him outside if he was sniffing, circling, or acting restless. Every time Snowy used the garden, he would receive fulsome praise and a small treat.

The little dog would be allowed in the living room when the family was home. If he became too exuberant, he would be removed from the room, but only for a maximum of two minutes time-out, and no grudges would be held against him once he was allowed back. He would have some playtimes and all meals in the kitchen. This would help him to develop a positive association with that room, instead of it being a place of isolation. The family and their friends would turn their backs if Snowy jumped up and would teach him to trade if he took anything of theirs.

Snowy needed some outlets for his energy, so he would have some new toys. Some could be left out for him to play with at will, and the others kept out of reach for special play rewards. He needed two daily walks of at least twenty minutes, and Barbara agreed to take him out more. As Snowy was so responsive, I suggested the children teach him some tricks. While I was there, Snowy learned to give a paw and sit up on his hind legs on request, and he looked very pleased with himself. The children were excited about teaching him, too.

Because Snowy had been so responsive that day, Barbara felt more positive about integrating him more closely into the family. It was heartwarming to hear, three days later, that Snowy's behavior had greatly improved. Several weeks later, Snowy had transformed into a polite, friendly dog who was a joy to be with. He had charmed the groomer and veterinarian during that time, and the children and their friends were proud of the new tricks he could do for them. This lovely little dog truly became part of the family—and they were all happier as a result.

EMMY: FEAR-AGGRESSION

Gabby, the owner of Emmy, a five-year-old Irish Setter, was sobbing so hard over the phone that I could barely make out the words. It turned out that Emmy had bitten a visiting cousin when he bent over to stroke her head. This had never happened before. The shocked cousin had told Gabby that Emmy was a dangerous dog and should be euthanized.

Gabby was devastated. Emmy had started life on a puppy farm, and Gabby and Keith had adopted her when she was a year old, as her previous owner couldn't cope with what she called Emmy's "neurotic" nature. Sadly, dogs born in these places often have issues because their start in life is appalling. Poor diet and hygiene, no medical care, very little socializing with people—the combination is a recipe for future behavior problems.

Gabby and Keith had carefully nurtured Emmy over the past four years, but in some ways they had overcompensated for her difficult past and they pandered to her a great deal. This is common in owners of dogs who were previously mistreated because the owners feel sorry for the dog. Explaining that dogs live in the moment and don't need to be treated like pieces of fragile crystal is something I have to do quite often. Emmy's nervous nature was constantly being reinforced because Gabby and Keith both made a huge fuss of her every time she showed signs of being anxious. This was exacerbating her problems rather than helping her to overcome them.

We discussed how the biting incident came about. Emmy is an extremely nervous dog, which is common when the socializing window of opportunity has been missed. Gabby's cousin hadn't listened when Gabby told him that Emmy got frightened if people approached her. Instead of giving her space, he strode over to Emmy (the worst thing you can do with a nervous dog), leaned over her (even scarier for her), and patted her heavily on the head. The bite was more like a nip, which resulted in a scratch and a few drops of blood, rather than a deep wound. This wasn't a dangerous dog—this was a very scared dog whose personal space had been rudely invaded.

When I visited, Emmy barked when the doorbell rang but shrank back as soon as Gabby let me in. We sat down and I paid no direct attention to Emmy at all but simply used peripheral vision to observe her. Gabby described how Emmy took her time to get to know people but was friendly once she felt safe with them. As we spoke, Emmy gradually moved closer until she was sniffing my hand. I kept my focus on Gabby, with occasional sideways glances at Emmy. After a few minutes, reassured, Emmy pushed her nose into my hand and looked up at me. Using slow, gentle movements, I stroked beneath her chin. With a sigh that signaled a release of stress, Emmy settled down to lie at my feet. She'd clearly decided that I was friend, not foe.

The consultation showed that Emmy needed three things: to have her need for personal space respected; to develop her confidence around people; and for Gabby and Keith to resist the urge to make so much fuss of her each time she looked anxious.

We made out an action plan. Irish Setters are beautiful dogs, and it's easy to understand why strangers would want to say hello. Gabby and Keith would ask people not to step toward, loom over, or touch Emmy. If their request was ignored, as with Gabby's cousin, they should step in between Emmy and the person, to block access to her. If necessary, they could even walk away.

If her owners insisted that Emmy's personal space was respected, this lovely but timid dog would gradually begin to feel more comfortable around strangers. This would enable Gabby and Keith to help Emmy cope when visitors arrived or if people stopped to chat while they were out. All visitors should be asked to move slowly, speak quietly, and avoid paying attention to Emmy unless she instigated contact. Even when Emmy approached them, guests should take care to be very gentle with her. The increased feeling of safety would tempt Emmy out of her shell, but it was likely that she would always be a shy dog because of her background.

By giving Emmy extra attention every time she started to look anxious, Gabby and Keith were heightening Emmy's feeling that there was something of which to be scared. I suggested that they simply touch her gently, just once, and carry on with what they were doing, saying nothing more than a quiet "It's okay." This would reassure Emmy without increasing her anxiety.

Two weeks later, Emmy was responding well. Her body language was more confident, and she clearly felt more secure. She was standing quietly, instead of stepping back, when people approached Gabby and Keith in the street. They made sure that no one invaded Emmy's space, and the increase in their dog's confidence impacted her relationships with visitors, too. A month later Emmy was moving forward to greet people with a softly wagging tail as they came through the door.

Since then, Emmy has gone from strength to strength. She'll never be an exuberant, outgoing dog—this isn't her nature—but she's comfortable in the presence of people now, even strangers.

BEAUTY: SEPARATION ANXIETY

Beauty was a three-year-old ex-racing Greyhound who had failed to make the grade as a racer. Her trainer had handed her in to a rescue shelter, so that she could have a comfortable retirement. Stella, who adopted Beauty, had fallen in love as soon as she saw her and had rather enjoyed having Beauty follow her every time she moved. Unfortunately, Beauty's attachment to her new owner quickly developed into intense neediness, and she chewed the soft furnishings and edge of the carpet whenever Stella had to leave her alone at home.

Observing them together revealed a very close mutual bond that Stella was deliberately encouraging and cultivating. Their affection for each other was touching, but Stella wasn't giving Beauty the tools she needed to be able to cope without her—and this wasn't fair to Beauty. Each time Stella moved around the room or went into another room, she glanced over at Beauty, who immediately got up to trail her. Stella was inadvertently setting Beauty up to suffer when she was left by herself, and this needed to change.

In future, Stella needed to give Beauty the space to remain where she was when Stella moved. This meant no eye contact or even glancing in Beauty's direction when Stella left the room. She needed to be casual about it, so that Beauty would learn that Stella could come and go without any need for Beauty to worry. She could enjoy the close relationship with Beauty by instigating playtimes and snuggle times together and could still have her beside her on the sofa and on the dog bed in her bedroom. But Stella needed to step back a little from acting so needy toward her dog. She would close doors behind her for just a few moments and then return through them. The leaving ritual of gathering her keys, phone, and purse was exacerbating Beauty's anxiety, so Stella would go through this without focusing on Beauty to gauge her reactions. Instead, she would repeatedly go through her ritual, exit the house, and then walk straight back indoors and sit down. Her time outside the house would be increased by a few more minutes each day.

Beauty, like most Greyhounds, liked to sleep a lot. Her favorite resting place was in Stella's bedroom, as her beloved owner's scent was strongest in there. We decided that Stella would leave her bedroom door open when she left the house, so that Beauty could have extra comfort from going to her room if she wished to.

This worked very well. When I next visited two weeks later, there were no fresh chewed edges on the carpet and the curtains were intact. Stella and Beauty both looked more relaxed, and Stella told me that Beauty was no longer displaying any signs of anxiety now that she could go in Stella's bedroom when left alone.

Humans and dogs can have unhealthily co-dependent relationships as easily as can humans and their own species. Through taking a step back from her own need for constant attention from her dog, Stella allowed the opportunity for a much healthier bond to develop, and both she and Beauty were happier as a result of this.

TOBY: FOOD-GUARDING AND DOG-AGGRESSION

Toby, a three-year-old Staffordshire Bull Terrier, went into foster care after being rescued from death row at a dog pound. We can never know the past of these dogs who have been deliberately abandoned or are found as strays, and we can only guess at what they have endured in the past. Toby had clearly been mistreated; he had numerous scars and he was very underweight.

This lovely boy needed some intensive help, and Di, his fosterer, was determined to do her best to rehabilitate him and prepare him for a forever home. Toby was gentle with people—unless they approached his food, in which case he would growl and posture until they backed away—and he had quickly developed a bond with Di.

Indoors, Toby's only issue was food-guarding. Outside, he would lunge, bark, and threaten any other dogs he saw. Otherwise he was a very sweet, friendly dog, who learned quickly and soaked up affection like a sponge. It was clear that there had been little love in his life before his rescue, as he craved approval and gentle touch and responded well to both. This desire to please and be loved would be the keys to helping Toby overcome his issues.

Both the food-guarding and dog-aggression would make it hard to re-home Toby successfully, and Di was aware that it would take consistent work on her part to get long-term results. Di and I discussed the rehabilitation plan, and she was keen to follow it through.

As Toby was underweight, it was likely that he had either been deliberately deprived of food in the past or had been unable to provide for himself as a stray dog. Food-guarding is a very common issue when a dog has gone hungry for long periods. As Toby was having two meals each day, morning and late afternoon, I suggested that Di teach Toby to sit and ask him to do this while she put his food bowl on the floor. He must not be expected to wait for his food, but sitting for just a moment would help him to calm down at mealtimes. Di was to then step right away from Toby while he ate and would casually walk past when he had finished his food and was snuffling at the empty bowl. As she passed she would throw a piece of chicken, cheese, or sausage into the bowl and keep on walking.

Within two days, Toby started waiting hopefully by his empty bowl. Di could approach close enough to drop a morsel into it, instead of throwing it from farther away, without any growling or "back off" signals from Toby. She then changed the "extra" food to a single piece of kibble and dropped that into Toby's bowl on alternate passes, then just added some kibble occasionally. There was no adverse reaction from Toby, and no signs of any return of the food-guarding. Toby had learned that people near his bowl were a bonus instead of a threat.

Toby's dog-aggression issue took longer to address, and we guessed that he may have previously been used for fighting or as a bait dog. He was antagonistic toward every dog he saw, even at a distance of several hundred yards, and would pull on his lead to get to them, barking and snarling. Toby meant business, and Di was almost pulled over several times. This made walks scary for her, as well as highly stressful for both of them. His rehabilitation needed to be a slow process, taken at a pace that he could comfortably cope with. Any pressure on Toby to get too close, too soon, would mean starting over at the beginning.

As Toby was on a collar and leash and was powerfully muscled despite his low weight, he was stronger than Di when he lunged forward. We put him in a padded fitted harness, as this gave Di more control when Toby pulled, and it also ensured that his neck wouldn't be damaged when he strained at the leash. Dogs can incur serious internal injuries if they experience strong pressure on the throat. As Toby's dog-aggression was so severe, we arranged for a friend to walk her very calm Labrador on the far side of a quiet field and took Toby there. As soon as he saw the dog he started to lunge and bark, so Di took him out of the field and waited until he was calmer before walking back through the entrance. After an hour of multiple exits and entrances, Toby was tolerating the presence of another dog in the distance and was happy to sniff around on his side of the field. Di praised him every time he focused on anything but the dog and gave him a ball to carry in his mouth.

Over the following two weeks, we took Toby to the field every day, gradually decreasing the distance between him and Di's friend's dog, and walking Toby in the opposite direction as soon as he started to react. The following week we could walk both dogs parallel to each other, and Toby even wagged his tail. We did this for several days before walking Toby behind the Labrador so that he could smell her without feeling threatened. Finally, we allowed the dogs to introduce themselves, and Toby made a new friend.

It took months before Toby could socialize with other new dogs, but patience and careful observation of his body language paid off. Eventually Toby went to his forever home, and his proud foster carer waved him off. He left without a backward glance, though Di shed some tears, and settled happily into his new home.

FREDDY: JUMPING UP AND MOUTHING

Freddy had been handed over to a rescue because his owners couldn't cope with him jumping at everyone and grabbing their arms and hands. This gorgeous German Shepherd was only nine months old when he was put in foster care, and all Freddy needed was some firm boundaries and to learn self-control.

A great many dogs are dumped or handed over during the adolescent stage because the cute, biddable little puppy suddenly gets a lot bigger and starts to act up. If they haven't been taught acceptable behavior, their exuberance can get out of hand—and this was the case with Freddy.

He was a lovely young dog—friendly, sociable, very intelligent—and it was clear he had no actual issues. He was simply excitable. Because he'd been allowed to get away with it as a puppy (and very often people will encourage this behavior in puppies, then don't like it when they grow up!), he couldn't understand why people were getting angry with him. Freddy would use his mouth while he was jumping, in order to get maximum attention—his body language shouted, "I'm delighted to see you—look at me!" He reminded me of a child tugging at his mother's hand and clothes, and there was clearly no malice in his behavior. However, it could be unnerving for humans who felt intimidated by a large dog leaping all over them.

It was very easy to teach Freddy polite manners. All his fosterers and their guests needed to do was to turn away from Freddy when he jumped up. This would teach him that jumping meant the loss of attention, instead of more attention. As Freddy had been told, "No," very loudly for so long that the word meant nothing to him, I asked his fosterers to try not to even speak to him while he was jumping. If they had to speak, it would be more effective to say a firm, calm "Off" instead. Folding their arms across their chests as they turned away meant that Freddy had nothing to grab onto. As soon as Freddy had all four paws on the ground, he should be rewarded with praise and a game or treat, with his fosterers taking care not to let him get overexcited—otherwise he would start jumping again.

When Freddy tried to lead someone by taking their hand or arm in his mouth, the best course of action was to squeal very loudly and walk away—even though he didn't use his teeth on them. The squeal would tell him that his behavior was out of line, and walking away from Freddy provided the opposite reaction to the one he was aiming to get: their attention.

We worked with Freddy, and he started to "get it" very quickly. While we did this, I pointed out the signals that Freddy was giving out just before he went to jump up. His body would tense to spring, and his ears were pricked in a state of alert awareness. His lolling tongue, so like a smile, showed that he meant no harm. He was being playful, but in ways that were unacceptable.

Freddy's fosterers watched for the early warning signs and immediately asked him to sit when they noticed him prepare to spring. Sitting is incompatible with jumping, and it calmed Freddy down instantly.

Happily, Freddy responded so quickly to these new boundaries that he didn't have to wait long for a new home!

BEAR: SETTLING IN AND HOUSE-TRAINING

Bear was a beautiful Rottweiler, thought to be around three years old. He had been found straying and taken to the dog pound. As he hadn't been microchipped and had no identity disk on his collar, it was hoped that his owner would search for him. However, no one came forward and Bear was taken to a rescue shelter to be assessed and rehomed. Luckily for Bear, he was only in kennels for a few days before a very sweet couple called Judy and Steve adopted him. They had lived with Rottweilers in the past, had been looking for another since their last dog had died, and were eager to take Bear home with them.

Judy called me the day before they were due to collect Bear, to discuss how to help him settle in smoothly. I'm always delighted when clients contact me when they're thinking of getting a dog or have just bought or adopted a new friend. The first few days together are especially important because during this time the foundations are being laid for the future relationship, and starting off right can help to avoid the likelihood of issues developing in the future.

We talked through the welcome home plans for Bear. Judy and Steve would bring him indoors on his lead and walk him through to the back garden to let him sniff around and eliminate before coming inside to explore the home. His comfortable new bed and a stack of food were ready, and there were some treats, chews, and toys set aside. I asked Judy and Steve to try not to overwhelm him by making too much fuss of him at first and to hold off from having many visitors for a few days, so that Bear could find his feet (or paws) in his new home without the additional stress of extra company. It can be hard to resist the urge to constantly reassure and give affection to a new dog, but it eases the transition if the dog doesn't feel that too many demands are being made on him while he's feeling anxious and insecure.

Bear settled in well and seemed very happy with his new adopters. They fell in love with him right from the start and were careful to give him the chance to adapt to the big change in his life.

A week later I had another call from Judy, asking for a visit. Everything was rosy except the toilet-training, which wasn't going well at all. Bear was using the kitchen as his bathroom, despite easy access to the garden.

The first thing I noticed was that they were using household bleach to clean up after Bear. This disinfects the floor and masks the scent for humans but doesn't eliminate all traces of the scent for a dog's highly sensitive nose. If any scent remains, the dog perceives this as a toilet area and so will go there again. I asked Judy and Steve to use a designated cleaner from the pet shop or to clean up using a solution of biological washing powder or liquid that they would normally use for their clothes—either of these would remove all traces of Bear's scent from the floor. The kitchen chairs, table, and side units within Bear's reach would also need to be cleaned in case there had been splashes.

On observing them with Bear, I could see that they weren't picking up on the body language he was using to show he needed to go outside. Bear got very restless, and they spoke reassuringly to him instead of immediately taking him outside. We made it into the garden in time! Because the door was open most of the day, Judy and Steve expected Bear to go out whenever he felt like it. However, he still hadn't made the connection between the garden and his bathroom, so I asked them to start at the beginning and call him outside after each drink, meal, or nap and if they saw him starting to pace. It was vital that they went with him, so they could praise and reward him as soon as he eliminated. Any accidents indoors should be cleaned up without comment. They agreed to follow through on the advice.

A week later I had a call from Steve. Bear had only had one accident indoors since my visit, and that was when he was on the phone, the door was closed, and he hadn't noticed that Bear was getting restless. Bear had figured it out!

LINDY: INCESSANT BARKING

Lindy was a two-year-old Saint Bernard whose owners, Ted and Brigit, were being driven to distraction by her constant barking. They told me it had been going on for several months. Ted and Brigit had tried shaking a tin of pebbles at Lindy, spraying her with water, and dropping a bunch of keys beside her, but none of these methods had worked. I wasn't surprised! These are all methods that aim to shock the dog into submission and are the opposite of the Sympatico method of getting the dog's cooperation so that he or she responds willingly.

Lindy certainly was a barker! I could hear her before I even approached the house. This sounded more like the complaints of a dog who was suffering from boredom, rather than one who was anxious or feeling a need to warn people away. She stood, still barking, behind Ted when he opened the door but quieted for a couple of minutes to greet me with a waggy tail when I entered the house. Then she went out to the garden to resume reminding the whole area of her presence.

Talking through the situation with Ted and Brigit, it was clear that the barking had started to become a serious problem when Brigit took a new part-time job that entailed being away from the house for four hours each weekday. Lindy, who had been with them since puppyhood, had never been left alone for more than two hours until that time, and she wasn't coping well. Brigit was leaving Lindy out in the garden when she went to work, as she was anxious there could be "accidents" indoors if Lindy stayed inside. As Lindy had a large outdoor kennel for shelter, she was as comfortable as they could make her—though I suspected that Lindy thought she was supposed to be on guard duty out there, and that this would exacerbate the barking. Further questioning revealed that Lindy spent a lot of time in the living room when they were home. As she had never toileted indoors, there didn't seem to be any cause for Brigit to worry.

Ted called Lindy inside and she responded immediately. As soon as she started barking, I held up my hand in the "stop" position and thanked and rewarded her when she paused for breath. Ted and Brigit took over with this, and soon the gaps between barking episodes were much longer. Ted gave her a rawhide chew, and Lindy calmed down and lay at his feet.

We discussed ways to help Lindy cope with being left. Ted and Brigit would let Lindy stay indoors and would let her out to toilet and then call her in and invite her to go on her bed before they went out. Some chew toys and a filled Kong would give Lindy something to do while she was alone, and they would leave an old T-shirt on her bed for extra reassurance. Leaving home would be low key, with no major fuss being made about it. If they wanted to know what Lindy did while they were out, they could set up a video recorder to play back later on.

I discovered that Lindy wasn't being taken for regular walks. This was contributing to her feelings of boredom, as dogs need the stimulation of other sounds, smells, and sights on a regular basis. Taking Lindy for twenty-minute walks twice daily would allow her to use her senses more and would be very good for her mentally as well as physically. Ted and Brigit agreed to try this for two weeks and then call me.

Two weeks later, Lindy was barking a lot less and was far more relaxed. The video recordings showed that she had paced a little during the first few days, then had settled on her bed and gone to sleep until she heard the car pulling up outside. By the middle of the first week, Lindy was playing with the Kong they left for her, then going straight to her bed and sleeping the time away. There were no "accidents" indoors, so Brigit could leave her without worrying about returning to a cleanup task.

After a month, Lindy was only barking when she heard something outside and when visitors arrived. Her owners were relieved and delighted!

ORLA: FROM CRUELTY TO COMPASSION

Orla, a beautiful nine-year-old white Greyhound with one gray ear, was brought to me by a fellow behaviorist, and within a few minutes of her arrival I had signed her adoption papers. Orla and her two daughters were what are termed "cruelty cases." They were rescued from horrific circumstances in Ireland and were listed as being the most traumatized dogs to be shipped over to the UK kennels that I visited regularly. They had been locked in a dark shed for a long time, deprived of food and human company, and doused in toxic sheep dip chemicals. Orla's fur was stained pink and falling out in clumps, she was distressingly thin, she had a mammary tumor—and the brightest eyes I'd ever seen. It was love at first sight for both of us.

Skye and Orla were introduced during a short walk and seemed happy to meet each other. As Orla had never lived in a home, I expected her to be hesitant about coming in—but she looked up at me, then looked at my front door, and her face lit up. It was as if she knew she had come home. As soon as the door opened, she leaped in, tail wagging; found her way into the living room; and lay down on one of the large dog cushions. Everything in her demeanor shouted joy at the prospect of "Home Sweet Home" and within an hour she was happily "roaching"—lying on her back with all four legs in the air in an attitude of total trust.

Our new arrival was a shock to Skye, who was well socialized but hadn't lived with another dog. Once he realized that Orla was here to stay, he ran out into the back garden, yipping with confusion. A few minutes later he ventured back indoors, went over to touch noses with her, and lay down beside her. From then onward they became inseparable.

Both dogs drank a lot during the first day. The stress of change, even positive change, makes dogs very thirsty, as they tend to pant more. Orla left clumps of soft white hair in her wake at every movement, and they drifted through the air like swansdown. I took her outside and gently groomed her, but she lost all her fur within the first week or so, and it took a while to grow back.

Toilet-training went well, right from the start. I called her into the garden frequently and rewarded her each time she obliged. We only had one "accident" and this was during the first night, when I woke to find Orla gently nudging me with her nose. I leaped out of bed to take her outside, but she didn't quite make it to the back door. It was impressive how, in just a few hours, this sweet elderly girl understood that the garden was the toilet area.

At first, Orla was an expert counter-surfer and food thief—unsurprising, as she had been starved over a long period and thought every meal may be her last. She was tall for a Greyhound—she could put her paws on my shoulders when she stood up on her hind legs—so kitchen surfaces posed no problems for her. Each time she went to help herself to food I was preparing, I quietly stepped sideways to block her. Each time she leaped forward to snaffle food from my dinner plate, I turned away and told her to lie on her bed. It took Orla just two days to figure out there was no point in carrying on with the behavior—though anyone foolish enough to leave food lying around unattended had only themselves to blame when she cleared the plate!

I had expected that it would take some time to settle Orla in and help her to recover from her traumas, but she was quick to offer her trust, and she made it abundantly clear that she was happy to be with us. Dogs live in the moment, and each of Orla's current moments were good—filled with love, comfort, and nourishing food. After a few days she learned to play, and it was utterly heartwarming to watch her and Skye dancing around each other in the garden.

A week after coming to live with us, Orla had surgery for the mammary tumor. When I brought her home afterward, Skye, who prefers his own bed and doesn't often snuggle up with other dogs, somehow knew that his new best friend was feeling frail. It brought tears to my eyes when he lay close by her and offered his back so that she could rest her head on his flanks while she slept.

Orla recovered quickly and put on weight, and a soft, shiny new coat gradually emerged. Passers-by always stopped to speak to her and Skye during our walks, and Orla's gentle manner and polite way of stepping forward to greet strangers made her an ambassador for Greyhounds. Several people contacted Greyhound rescue organizations and adopted dogs because of our gentle girl.

Orla only lived for ten more months before a brain tumor stole her away from us. When she lost her vision and hearing, her pain medication was no longer keeping her comfortable, and she started suffering from seizures, I had no choice but to make the heartbreaking decision to let her go. Even to her final day, Orla's tail wagged as she lay beside me and rested her head in my lap. She had crept so deeply into all of our hearts, and we missed her terribly. For weeks afterward Skye lay on Orla's favorite sofa as a way of staying close to her, and I waited until he returned to his usual cheerful self before fostering other dogs.

This may seem a sad tale for a success story, yet it illustrates how quickly and easily dogs can let go of even the most difficult past. Orla was very special—not only to us, but also to every person who met her. The ease with which she adapted to a completely different lifestyle, her ability to find joy in each moment, even when seriously ill, and her generous demonstration of the gift of loving gentleness made her one of my greatest teachers.

SHEP: AGORAPHOBIA

Shep ("The Shepster"), who you met briefly at the beginning of chapter 6: "Who's Training Whom?," is on permanent foster with me, so will spend the rest of his life as a member of our family. He was considered unsuitable for rehoming for several reasons. The Shepster is a fifteen-year-old Collie-Husky crossbreed, a gorgeous cuddly bear of a dog, and his health issues include severe arthritis, seriously atrophied muscles on his back legs, liver failure, and an inoperable tumor. He was also agoraphobic and hadn't been walked for twelve years because of his terror of being outside.

Oldies Club, one of the rescue charities I'm involved with, takes in and rehomes dogs over the age of seven. I foster dogs for them and am very committed to promoting the joys of adopting an elderly dog—they have given a lifetime of love and devotion and deserve the best that life can offer during their twilight years.

The Shepster came to me when his owner had to go into sheltered accommodation and wasn't allowed to take him with her. When Shep arrived, it seemed likely that we would only have his company for a few weeks before he passed on. The aim was to keep him as comfortable as possible and to make sure that he was surrounded by love.

A very frail dog gazed appealingly at me when he arrived—and then he saw Skye! His tail seemed like an independent body part as it wagged with enthusiasm behind very wobbly legs. The Shepster, it seemed, absolutely loved doggy company! Skye immediately made it clear he was willing to take on the role of mentor, tutor, encourager, and playmate to his new friend.

During the first two days, Shep needed a lot of help to even get out of the back door into the garden. He's a heavily built dog, and Amber and I had to lift him together quite a few times when he landed flat on his chest. But The Shepster is a determined old gentleman, and by the third day he had learned to bunny-hop over the back step and could go in and out at will, with only occasional help. Knowing that Skye was playing in the garden gave Shep the motivation to get out there, and it was important that Shep's hind leg muscles were strengthened through very gentle exercise.

After a week, when Shep was a little stronger, I clipped on his leash and took him just outside the garden gate, onto the lane that leads to woods behind my house. Shep panicked and stumbled back into the garden as fast as his unsteady legs would carry him. I shut the gate and let him go back indoors. The following day we tried again, but this time I took Skye as well. Shep seemed more relaxed and took a few steps. I let him sniff around for a couple of minutes and then brought him back into the garden before he had a chance to become anxious.

This became a daily routine, and each day The Shepster went a little further and was steadier on his legs. I took things at a pace that Shep was comfortable with and observed him for any signs of tension so that he never felt under pressure to go farther than he wanted. After a while I took him alone, after Skye had his twice daily walks, and Shep got into the habit of waiting by the back gate for me to put on his leash as soon as I returned with Skye. The first time he did this felt like a major breakthrough!

A month after coming to live with us, The Shepster was walking more easily and could even run. Now he thoroughly enjoys going out into the big wide world and discovering the pleasures of fresh scents, new people, and other dogs. He's an absolute joy to live with and has developed a mischievous character. His latest escapade was to stage a breakout and take himself off to visit one of my neighbors—an extraordinary achievement, considering how terrified he was of the outside world. He's a very different dog to the sad, infirm soul who first arrived at our home, and it's a good feeling to see him making the most of life at last.

Bibliography

Bradshaw, John. *In Defence of Dogs: Why Dogs Need Our Understanding.* London: Allen Lane, 2011.

Clothier, Suzanne. *Bones Would Rain from the Sky: Deepening Our Relationships with Dogs.* New York: Warner Books, 2002.

Coppinger, Raymond, and Lorna Coppinger. *Dogs: A Startling New Understanding of Canine Origin, Behavior, and Evolution.* New York: Scribner, 2001.

Donaldson, Jean. *The Culture Clash.* Berkeley, CA: James & Kenneth, 1996.

Eaton, Barry. *Dominance in Dogs: Fact or Fiction?* Wenatchee, WA: Dogwise, 2010.

Horowitz, Alexandra. *Inside of a Dog: What Dogs See, Smell, and Know.* New York: Scribner, 2009.

Lowry, Rosie, and Marilyn Aspinall. *Understanding the Silent Communication of Dogs.* Coleshill, Warwickshire, UK: Lowry Industries Ltd., 2010.

McGreevy, Paul. *The Modern Dog's Life: How to Do the Best for Your Dog.* New York: The Experiment, 2010.

Rugaas, Turid. *My Dog Pulls. What Do I Do?* Wenatchee, WA: Dogwise, 2005.

————. *On Talking Terms with Dogs.* Wenatchee, WA: Dogwise, 2006.

Sheldrake, Rupert. *Dogs That Know When Their Owners Are Coming Home: And Other Unexplained Powers of Animals.* New York: Three Rivers Press, 2011.

Spiers, Winkie. *How to Handle Living with Your Dog.* Stratford on Avon, Warwickshire, UK: Short Stack Publishing, 2009.

Index

About the Author

Lisa Tenzin-Dolma is a canine psychologist and the author of fourteen books and more than five hundred published magazine articles. She is the director of the International School of Canine Psychology and the founder of The Dog Helpline. An active member of the Association of INTO Dogs, an organization for trainers and behaviorists who promote compassionate methods of working with dogs, Lisa is advisor to many rescue shelters. She works with all breeds of dogs and specializes in rehabilitating rescue dogs. Lisa offers pet lovers three websites: Her personal website: www.tenzindolma.co.uk; The Dog Helpline: www.thedoghelpline.com; and The International School of Canine Psychology: www.theiscp.com.

Notes

INTRODUCTION

1. Raymond and Lorna Coppinger, *Dogs: A Startling New Understanding of Canine Origin, Behavior, and Evolution* (New York: Scribner, 2001).
2. Jennifer A. Leonard , Robert K. Wayne , Jane Wheeler , Raúl Valadez , Sonia Guillén, and Carles Vilà, " Ancient DNA Evidence for Old World Origin of New World Dogs," *Science* 298, no. 5598 (22 November 2002): 1613–16.
3. Lyudmila N. Trut, "Early Canid Domestication: The Farm-Fox Experiment," *American Scientist* 87 (March–April 1999).
4. John Bradshaw, *In Defence of Dogs: Why Dogs Need Our Understanding* (London: Allen Lane, 2011).

2. INSTINCTS AND SENSES

1. K. Uvnas-Moberg, "Oxytocin May Mediate the Benefits of Positive Social Interaction and Emotions," *Psychoneuroendocrinology* 23, no. 8 (November 1998): 819–35.
2. Rupert Sheldrake, *Dogs That Know When Their Owners Are Coming Home: And Other Unexplained Powers of Animals* (New York: Three Rivers Press, 2011).
3. Information on articles and papers is at www.sheldrake.org/Research/morphic/.

3. BODY LANGUAGE AND COMMUNICATION

1. Televised for the Horizon program *The Secret Life of the Dog*, 2010.

4. HOW YOUR DOG READS YOU

1. Kun Guo, Daniel Mills, Kerstin Meints, Charlotte Hall, and Sophie Hall, "Left Gaze Bias in Humans, Rhesus Monkeys and Domestic Dogs," *Animal Cognition* (2008): 409–18.